The ESTUARY FLYFISHER

STEVE RAYMOND

Frank Amato
PORTLAND, OREGON

IN MEMORY OF
ED FOSS
TRUE FRIEND AND FELLOW ANGLER,
WHO INTRODUCED ME TO
THE MYSTERIES AND MAGIC OF ESTUARY FLY FISHING

Published in 1996 by Frank Amato Publications, Inc.
(503) 653-8108

Photographs by Joan and Steve Raymond (except where otherwise credited)
Flies photographed by Jim Schollmeyer
Book design and layout: Tony Amato

Softbound ISBN: 1-57188-060-7   UPC: 0-66066-00252-5
Hardbound Limited Edition ISBN: 1-57188-061-5   UPC: 0-66066-00253-2

1 3 5 7 9 10 8 6 4 2

PRINTED IN HONG KONG

CONTENTS

ACKNOWLEDGEMENTS

Many institutions and individuals provided generous assistance during the research for this book, and to all of them I offer grateful thanks:

—To the always helpful and efficient staff of the Fisheries Library at the University of Washington. Over the years the names and faces have changed, but the tradition of good service has continued.

—To the equally helpful and courteous staff of the National Oceanic and Atmospheric Administration Library at Sand Point, Seattle.

—To the National Ocean Survey's Pacific Operations Group at Sand Point, especially Duane Timmons and Dave Jones.

—To John Crocker and the other members of the Lower Umpqua Flycasters, plus all the other participating organizations, fisheries biologists, researchers, managers, and anglers who made the first Sea-Run Cutthroat Symposium in Reedsport, Oregon, such a resounding success.

—To my daughter, Stephanie, of People for Puget Sound, Seattle, for her valuable suggestions regarding the content of the chapter on the natural history of estuaries.

—To my son, Randy, for his helpful advice on how to report the results of my one-man, 18-year experiment in tracking movements of sea-run cutthroat at different stages of the tide, and for tying some of the flies pictured in this book.

—And to the countless anglers with whom I have fished and from whom I have gleaned insights over the years. There are too many to list, and some whose names I do not even know, but I consider all of them my friends and value my association with them, however brief or long it may have been. I hope to renew each acquaintance in the magical setting of an estuary.

—*Steve Raymond*
December, 1995

The river has come home. From its origins high in the hills it has made its way swiftly down the wooded slopes and forged a twisting path across the coastal plain, growing ever larger with the flow of many small tributaries, until now at last it has reached this place where it mingles with the sea. In the course of its passage it has collected soil and silt from countless forests and fields and brought them to this place, and here, in its final act as a river, it deposits them at its mouth, building a shallow apron at the margins of the tide. Over this gentle shelf the river goes home to the sea, not in any last spectacular display of strength, but simply as a broad flow of current that eases into the salt water with only a brief ripple of angry turbulence to mark its passage.

The place where all this happens is an estuary, and it is different from any other place on land or sea. An estuary offers a garden of life more rich and varied than the most fertile field or verdant rain forest, a vast array of animals and plants and even a few creatures that appear to share the attributes of both, a layered society of life that reaches from the muck of the bottom to the highest margins of the tide, a community of both permanent and transient members.

Probably it was in the estuaries that life took its first small, tentative steps from sea onto land, and now the estuaries are busy interchanges where the traffic of oceans mingles with the traffic of rivers, where migratory fish come and go in their appointed seasons and their offspring find food and protection among swarms of other fish that seldom leave the estuary.

In every climate, at every latitude, and in every season, estuaries offer an abundance of opportunities for anglers. Some—especially the estuaries of the Atlantic and Gulf Coasts—are well known to fishermen, but the estuaries of the Pacific Northwest are one of the last great fly-fishing frontiers. From Northern California to Southeast Alaska, the bulk of the West Coast's human population lives on or near estuaries, yet anglers from those population centers traditionally have looked mostly to inland lakes and streams for sport, leaving the estuaries only lightly fished. Only now are fly fishers beginning to understand the opportunities that exist in the estuaries. Those opportunities include salmon, cutthroat, steelhead, and Dolly Varden that come seasonally to the estuaries, and other species, such as sea perch and rockfish, that are resident throughout the year. With such a menu, there is never a time when estuaries are not worth fishing.

Even in winter, when the trout streams of sunshine fishermen are running dark and cold, there are steelhead and cutthroat moving in the estuaries. Later, in the spring, when the tiny swarming hosts of salmon fry begin their seaward migration, hungry cutthroat and Dolly Varden cluster off the river-mouths to wait for them. Estuarine food stocks reach their peak in summer and there is always a wealth of organisms for fly fishers to imitate, not to mention an abundance of sea perch, flounder, rockfish, cutthroat, and other species waiting to take those imitations. Early summer also brings the first salmon, with bright fish entering the outer estuaries as they start the final lap of their long homeward journey.

In late summer and early fall the cutthroat make their annual transit through the estuaries to the rivers, and the salmon quickly follow—first the pinks in August or September, then the cohos in October, finally the chum salmon that run from November all the way through until January in some locations. And by the time the last late-run chum salmon has spawned upstream and spent itself, the winter steelhead run will be well under way in the estuaries.

Great schools of sea perch wander the estuaries at any season, in search of food along the mudflats or amid forests of old pilings, and these often overlooked fish provide marvelous sport for anglers familiar with their virtues. Evenings in the estuaries sometimes bring rockfish to feed along rocky shoals or jetties, and these stubborn, hard-fighting fish are another worthy foe. Flounder lurk year-round like trapdoor spiders in the sandy estuary bottoms, and other species come and go throughout the year.

Yet even with this abundance of fish, estuaries are rarely crowded even while rivers and lakes are often jammed with anglers. There are seasonal exceptions—crowds form quickly when word gets around that the salmon are in—but for most of the year it is possible to fish the estuaries in nearly complete solitude, a virtue now lacking from most other angling venues.

> A broad flow of current . . . eases into the salt water with only a brief ripple of angry turbulence to mark its passage.

With so many potential rewards, it's puzzling there are not more estuary anglers. Perhaps one reason is that few people yet realize the quality of sport that estuaries have to offer; in all the expansive literature of angling, there are few useful mentions of such fishing, fewer still of estuary fishing in the Pacific Northwest. The very abundance and diversity of estuarine life may be another discouraging factor; a healthy estuary holds such a wide variety of life that a person can scarcely hope to learn to identify all that he or she may see. The daunting complexities of fishing estuaries—the need for understanding of their conformation and currents, the subtle interrelationships and habits of their many forms of life, and all the tricky nuances of weather, time, and tide—also may deter some anglers. Yet these very complexities are among the greatest charms of estuary fishing, a challenge to be welcomed rather than avoided

Even more than rivers, estuaries offer an ever-changing environment. They are not the same as rivers or lakes, yet they combine some of the features of both, plus others that are unique. They come in all sizes, from very small to very large; there are estuaries within estuaries, simple estuaries and complex estuaries, estuaries where fresh water sometimes predominates and others where the opposite is true. No two estuaries are exactly the same, yet all share at least some of the same characteristics.

The tide is the principal factor that makes estuary fishing different from any other type of angling. Once or twice each day the tide drains the estuary and then refills it, and each flood tide is a form of renewal, bringing food to those animals and plants that must sit and wait for it to come, bringing also fish that can follow the tide in pursuit of the food it carries. In its turn, each ebb tide offers temporary respite from the cycle of feeding or being fed upon, of being predator or prey. A rising river is another form of renewal, bringing the estuary a fresh supply of minerals, salts, and nutrients leached from the inland rock and soil, adding to the wealth already stored in the sea.

When the ebbing tide nears the end of its farthest retreat, broad expanses of the estuary are left exposed—sandbanks and mudflats, smooth and wet and darkly streaked with straggling little streams draining the last water from the remotest margins of the bay. This is the best time to study an estuary, to see all its component parts revealed and to make note of the sandbars, snags, and channels that are always hidden by the higher tides. All the varied layers of estuary life are then visible, from the yellowing ranks of saltwort at the tide's upper grasp to the oysters clustered on the lower flats like jagged shards of glass. A single shallow channel carries away the last of the tide and the flow of the river that feeds the estuary; otherwise, only isolated tidal pools remain.

All is quiet when the tide reaches its ebb. Even the barnacles have withdrawn their tiny fernlike wands, waiting for the return of the tide before they begin waving in the current once again. The diving ducks and grebes have followed the tide's retreat, leaving only gulls and fish crows to scavenge among the flotsam left drying on the flats. Sandpipers run along on blurred feet, leaving tiny fossil-like tracks in their wake, then take flight in tight flocks that twist and turn with miraculous synchronization. Farther out, in deeper water, brilliant urchins and bright starfish lie motionless among sand-dollar clusters, and lush beds of eelgrass bend gracefully in the gentle current of the outward flow.

The tide turns slowly and subtly. The first visible sign of change is a gentle reversal in the direction of the waving eelgrass strands, as they swing about in obedience to the inward flow. Then the moving edge of the rising tide begins to slide softly up the sandy slopes and fill the lowest spots on the outer flats. The tide picks up speed and begins spilling over sandbars into stagnant pools, and with the first rush of cold, oxygenated water, the pools suddenly come alive with the quick rise of a cutthroat, or the sudden flashing turn of a school of sea perch, or perhaps the leap of a steelhead that has been waiting for the tide's return. With the first incoming wavelet, the barnacles reach out again to begin their waving search for food, and a chattering kingfisher drops from a shoreline maple to pluck a single luckless candlefish from a school that has left its wake of tiny dimples on the surface of the tide.

What began slowly and subtly suddenly becomes swift and strong, and the tide builds to a powerful surge that sweeps in over the flats and bars with a current like a mighty river. It reaches out to fill every cul-de-sac and corner of the estuary, racing up the beach toward the line of drying flotsam left by the last high water. It lifts strands of weed growing among the gravel and restores them to movement, stirs the pillbugs, shrimps, snails, and worms from their hiding places, and laps around dark old wooden pilings with their clustered colonies of clinging life. Occasionally the moving crest betrays the fleeting glimpse of a great fish making its way back to the river, a shadowy form intent upon its purpose, and sometimes the glassy surface is broken by a leaping fish whose circle of re-entry is erased quickly by the restless movement of the tide.

This is how it is in the estuaries, where I often fish alone. But I am never lonely here, for in addition to the gulls and grebes and kingfishers, I have always the company of the estuary's other regular inhabitants—cormorants and herons, ospreys and eagles, sometimes seals or otters, and all the teeming, hopping, crawling, burrowing life of the beaches. And of course the fish, always the fish, a dozen different species at a time, coming or going, feeding or resting, traveling singly or in schools, hugging the bottom or knifing through the glistening surface, always there, always watchful, nearly always eager to accept a fly.

In the estuaries there is a curious sense of both distance and intimacy, of silence and sound, of stillness and movement, all somehow conveying the feeling of a primal place, a place close to the origin of things. Here stands revealed more of the natural scheme of things than can be glimpsed anywhere else on earth, and here the angler discovers his own minor role as a bit player on the vast natural stage, a single small spark of life lost among many, just another traveler on the tide, surrounded by the endless sea and the sky. Estuaries have the ability both to humble and inspire, and to renew the spirit even on days when the fish are few.

In the estuaries I can taste the sea-salt on my lips and feel the sea-wind in my hair. I can hear the gulls singing their haunting songs while I watch the swelling tide and search for the gleaming turn of a feeding fish. The fish will come, as they almost always do when the tide is running; a long cast, parallel to the flow, and the bright fly will sweep and tumble in the current until suddenly a fish is there to take it strongly.

These moments make worthwhile all the time spent exploring, watching, learning, and trying to understand the secrets of the estuaries and all their strong, quick life. Those secrets—some of them, anyway—are the subject of this book.

The word "estuary" is derived from the Latin word *aestis,* meaning tide. Usually it is applied to any place where a river or stream enters salt water. By this definition, even the outfall of a tiny brook, swallowed quickly in the vastness of the sea, is a miniature estuary; but so also are the broad inland bays and sounds that dot the Northwest coast all the way from Washington's midpoint to Southeast Alaska, fed by scores of rivers. Even open coastal waters are considered estuaries if they are diluted by freshwater runoff. The truth is that there is no precise, commonly accepted definition of an estuary.

This is not due to any lack of effort to devise one. Over the years, scientists have proposed various all-encompassing definitions in hopes of arriving at one that could be adopted as a standard, but none has yet achieved universal acceptance. One difficulty is that the boundaries of estuaries are defined more by salinity than geography, and since the saline boundaries of most estuaries change constantly, the size and shape of an estuary is a perpetually moving target—which makes it a very difficult thing to define. For an angler's purposes, however, any partly enclosed body of salt water—a bay, inlet, channel, tidal passageway, or sound—with an opening to the sea, fed by one or more streams with sufficient volume to dilute seawater and influence the behavior of fish beyond the mouth of the stream, may be considered an estuary.

This is a broad definition. At one end of the scale it includes such huge estuaries as Chesapeake Bay, Puget Sound, and San Francisco Bay, plus all the smaller estuaries within them; at the other it may include places where even the tiniest trickle of fresh water, or sometimes even seepage over a beach, reaches the sea—for I have seen examples where these were sufficient to influence the behavior of fish in salt water.

A classic case is a little stream my fishing companions and I call "Mini Creek" because it is so small, carrying so little water even at peak flow that it could scarcely wet a boot. It is far too small to support a run of fish of any kind, but where it reaches salt water there are nearly always sea-run cutthroat gathered off its mouth to feed, and one day I watched a chum salmon beat itself to death in a vain attempt to swim up the creek's tiny flow. The salmon obviously had strayed from its native stream, but the tiny discharge of Mini Creek had caught its attention and influenced its behavior—in this case, fatally.

Each estuary, regardless of its size or nature, provides a unique fishery. The species of fish sought by anglers may vary from one estuary to another, or from one season to another, and so may the tactics used to catch them; even when the same species of fish are present in different estuaries, their behavior may vary in response to the unique characteristics of each estuary, including water temperature, tides, currents, and other factors. For these reasons, estuary fly fishers must always be prepared to adapt their tactics to meet local conditions.

Experienced freshwater anglers know that success depends upon knowledge of the stream, of its insects and other forage species, the places where it holds trout, and how these places may change from time to time because of winter floods, storms, or routine fluctuations in the flow of the river. The same sort of intimate knowledge is critical to angling success in estuaries, but there is even more to learn. Different seasons may bring different species of gamefish to the estuary, and these fish may behave differently at different stages of the tide; the same is true of the forage fish and other creatures that provide gamefish with food. The very shape and contour of an estuary may change from year to year, or even from one season to the next, according to the whims of wind and tide and flood. It takes patient study to learn an estuary well, to understand its complex web of life, to know when it is likely to hold fish, what kind, and where, and how best to take them on the fly.

The number of recognized different types of estuaries is relatively small, but the things that go on in them are amazingly complex, and there are always more of these than easily meet the eye. The following discussion bypasses many of these complexities to focus on matters of most interest to anglers; those who wish to know more about the complex internal mechanics of estuaries are referred to the sources listed in the bibliography.

The Umpqua River estuary in Oregon, a classic example of a "drowned rivermouth" type of estuary.

Types of Estuaries

Many estuarial basins are the direct or indirect result of glacial action. During the last age of glaciation, water evaporated from the sea and fell as snow over the continents, freezing into vast ribbons of ice that held the water and kept it from returning to the sea. This caused the sea level to drop, uncovering coastal plains and forcing rivers to run farther to reach the sea. Eventually, when the glaciers began melting and releasing their stored-up water back to the sea, the oceans rose and inundated the valleys the rivers had cut for themselves through the coastal plains. These flooded basins became many of the estuaries that are familiar shapes on our modern maps.

Some of these estuaries are large and complicated, with ragged, irregular shorelines, a result of many tributaries having joined to erode softer soil and rock. Chesapeake Bay is a classic example of this type of estuary, with its broad, sprawling expanse of water fed by many sluggish rivers. In other cases, only a single large river was involved, or the rock was made of sterner stuff so that rivers joined to force only a single channel through it; when the sea rushed in, it flooded the straight and narrow valley thus created. The Hudson River estuary on the Atlantic Coast is one example of this type of "drowned rivermouth" estuary; the Umpqua River estuary on the Pacific Coast is another.

Other estuaries were formed directly by the great weight and grinding action of the glacial ice itself, which often crept down the course of an existing river and carved deep chasms, stopping only at the edge of the sea. Frequently the fissures thus formed were below sea level, so when the glaciers began to retreat the ocean quickly spilled in and flooded the deep scars they left behind. Now we call them fjords, and they are found in many places—the Norwegian coast, the spectacular west coast of New Zealand's South Island, the ragged coastline of British Columbia, and the maze of deep waterways called Puget Sound and Hood Canal. In Alaska, the glacial process of creating fjord-type estuaries is still under way.

But glaciers were not alone in forming the shapes of estuaries. Silt swept down by rivers through ages of erosive action, then slowly sculpted by winds and tides, has created barriers, spits or islands off the mouths of many streams; these barriers, in turn, restrict the free exchange of water from inside the barrier to the sea beyond, forming enclosed estuaries such as Corpus Christi Bay in Texas and many of the smaller estuaries of the Northern California and Southern Oregon coasts.

Violent earth movements also have sometimes been responsible for creating estuaries. Tomales Bay, north of San Francisco, is an example; there a section of earth between two faults slipped below the level of the surrounding land and allowed the sea to enter.

An estuary shaped by one of these natural processes may contain smaller estuaries shaped by another. Puget Sound, for example, was created primarily by glacial action, but many of the streams flowing into the sound have since formed their own distinctive estuaries, bounded by sand spits or deltas made from cargoes of silt eroded from the surrounding hillsides and mountains.

There are remarkable differences in the types of estuaries found along the Pacific Coast. Since the coasts of

"Mini Creek," an estuary so small it's hardly visible. But the fish know it's there.

California and Oregon largely escaped the spectacular scarring and sculpting of glacial action, estuaries in these states are mostly of the drowned rivermouth type, often with the added features of sand spits, deltas, or brackish lagoons at the river's mouth. Estuaries of this type tend to be much smaller and less complicated than estuaries created by glacial action. In fact, Oregon has only about 300 miles of coastline, including all its estuaries, while Washington has nearly 2,350 miles, including glacial-carved Puget Sound, Hood Canal, and the Strait of Juan de Fuca. British Columbia, with its maze of convoluted glacial-sculpted waterways and hundreds of estuaries along the Inside Passage, has 16,200 miles. These comparisons make it clear that from an angler's standpoint, the greatest opportunities for estuary fishing are along the northern coast, where most landforms, and most estuaries, bear the distinctive marks of glacial action.

Regardless of their type or where they are located, all estuaries are inherently ephemeral. Over time they fill with sediment and silt, so that eventually—barring geological cataclysm or changes in sea level—they migrate seaward, leaving behind meadows or salt marshes. Usually this process takes place too slowly for humans to notice, but in estuaries with exceptionally heavy sediment loads the changes may be quite evident—and quite dramatic—within the span of a few years.

Dams also can change the topography and ecology of an estuary by restricting the flow of silt and sediment down the river that feeds it. In some cases this can lead to the erosion or disappearance of sand spits or bars built from sediment transported by the river in its natural state, and this in turn may change the whole shape and structure of the estuary. Such changes may become visible within a few years after a dam is erected.

Construction of jetties, breakwaters, or other structures also can change local patterns of silt deposition or circulation in an estuary and affect its topography, although the changes usually are not as sweeping or dramatic as those resulting from a dam.

Water Circulation in Estuaries

Estuaries are classified not only by the geological forces that created them, but also by the type of water circulation that takes place in them—for although a river's entry to the sea may appear smooth and simple on the surface, the interface between fresh and salt water is in reality often complex and changing.

One reason is that salt water has a greater density than fresh water and the two do not mix readily; fresh water from a river always tends to form a distinct layer on top of salt water. The degree of mixing that does take place depends on circulation within the estuary, and this in turn depends on the shape of the estuary, its tidal range, the volume of fresh water entering into it, winds, and other variables. Where circulation is thorough and rapid, fresh and salt water mix quickly and become homogeneous in salinity, temperature, and oxygen content; but where it is sluggish, slow, or lacking altogether, fresh and salt water remain in separate layers, each with sharply different measures of salinity, temperature, and oxygen.

The measured distance between maximum ebb and maximum flood tide is known as the tidal range, and where it is large and the shape and contours of the estuary encourage strong tidal currents to develop, circulation is usually good, with a thorough blending of fresh and salt water. Where the tidal range is smaller and the shape or conformation of the estuary does not lend itself to formation of swift currents, circulation is likely to be poor

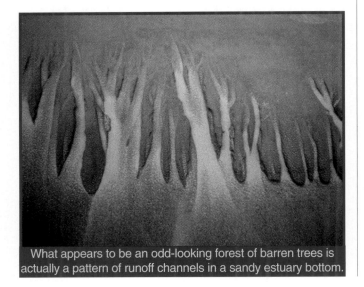
What appears to be an odd-looking forest of barren trees is actually a pattern of runoff channels in a sandy estuary bottom.

and fresh and salt water will remain unmixed, or poorly mixed at best.

The amount of fresh water entering an estuary usually changes seasonally. Northern rivers receive runoff from seasonal rains or melting snow in late spring or early summer and may swell in volume to the point where they force all the salt water out of the estuary into which they drain; when that happens, obviously no mixing can occur within the estuary. On the other hand, winter freezes or the hot, dry weather of late summer may reduce the flow of rivers to the point where they provide little measurable dilution; at such times the estuarial waters may be nearly as salty as the open sea itself, and again there is little or no mixing. At other seasons, a moderate sustained flow of fresh water may allow some circulation and good mixing, depending on the tidal range of the estuary and the strength of the currents within it.

Patterns of circulation also may be disrupted seasonally by wind. High winds generate waves that accelerate the mixing process; they also may either enhance or retard tidal flows (prevailing winds are one of many factors used in forecasting local tides). Winds have their greatest impact in broad, shallow estuaries where sustained gales may churn the entire water column so even silt from the bottom is lifted into suspension; the shallow "toe" of boot-shaped Hood Canal is one place where this happens occasionally.

Estuaries in the far north may freeze for long periods during winter. The ice cover keeps the wind from having its usual impact on circulation and may even restrict established tidal channels so normal mixing patterns are disturbed. In the spring, when the ice breaks up and melts, it leaves a layer of fresh or brackish water on the surface—water that is slow to mix because of its lighter density.

Stratification—layers of fresh water forming on top of salt—occurs most often in estuaries with a strong freshwater inflow, low sediment discharge, and small tidal range. Under these circumstances, the lighter fresh water spreads like a thin blanket over the surface of the estuary, flowing slowly seaward; sea water pushed by the rising tide penetrates under the lighter layer and is driven inland like a wedge toward the mouth of the river. A stable gradient forms between the layers of water, which differ markedly in density and salinity; this gradient is known as the halocline. However, because the freshwater layer is moving over salt water, shear stress can occur at the interface, creating turbulence and generating internal waves that break through the halocline and allow small quantities of salt water to penetrate the freshwater layer. British Columbia's Fraser River estuary is an example of this so-called "salt wedge" type of estuary. In far northern climes, estuaries of this type are more likely than others to become icebound in winter because the freshwater surface layer freezes more readily than sea water.

In estuaries with a greater tidal range or smaller freshwater inflow, more mixing can occur. Tidal currents are strong enough to move the whole water mass up or down the estuary, and in addition to shear stress at the halocline, this movement also creates friction between the water and the bed of the estuary, generating turbulence and contributing to the mixing of fresh and salt water. Chesapeake Bay and parts of the Strait of Juan de Fuca are examples of such moderately stratified or partly mixed estuaries.

Tillamook Bay is one of the largest estuaries on the Oregon coast; this view is near the bay's narrow mouth. The boats are filled with salmon anglers.

In broad, shallow estuaries where tides are very strong, or are enhanced by prevailing winds, the mixing of fresh and salt water may be so complete there is no measurable difference from surface to bottom. However, while vertical mixing may be complete, there may still be differences in horizontal circulation due to the Coriolis force, caused by the earth's rotation. In larger estuaries of the Northern Hemisphere, the Coriolis force causes salt water to move on the left and lighter fresh or brackish water to flow on the right. In the Southern Hemisphere the horizontal circulation is in the opposite direction. (A more detailed explanation of the Coriolis force will be found later in the chapter on tides.)

Fjord-type estuaries are governed by yet another set of rules. Fresh water flowing into the fjord forms the usual surface layer and moves slowly toward the estuary mouth; the sea's entry often is restricted by a shallow rim at the mouth, and salt water spilling over the rim and into the fjord slides under the fresh water layer. The high, precipitous walls of many fjords prevent wind from aiding the mixing or circulation of water, and the estuary becomes sharply layered throughout its length and depth. Because there is limited circulation and lack of exchange, over time the deeper water of the fjord becomes sluggish and is robbed of its oxygen content by the decay of organic materials drifting down from the upper layers where life abounds. This process, similar to eutrophication in lakes, eventually may make the depths of the fjord inhospitable to life. These same circumstances also make deep, sheltered fjords especially vulnerable to pollution; because of the slow and limited circulation, it may take years for any polluting agent to be completely flushed away.

There are other types of estuaries with circulations that defy easy classification. In some, wind is more important than either tidal action or freshwater inflow. In others, local features shape the circulation pattern so parts of the estuary are completely mixed while others are stratified. Conditions in either type may fluctuate rapidly depending on the state of the wind or tide.

Estuarine Life

Regardless of the degree of mixing that takes place within them, most estuaries act as nutrient traps. Rivers flowing toward the sea gather salts and minerals from soil and bedrock and organic materials from the decay of forests and swamps, and all these are combined in a rich broth carried by the current until it meets the tide. The tide brings its own share of the sea's great store of minerals and salts, collected from ages of runoff by countless rivers and concentrated by evaporation. In this fashion the wealth of both land and sea are blended in the contending waters of the estuary, creating an abundant supply of raw materials for life, and this is what makes estuaries so biologically active.

Were it not for this abundance of nutrients, it is unlikely so many forms of life would have gone through the evolutionary struggle necessary to adapt to estuarine habitats—for plants and animals in estuaries must contend with more rapidly changing and extreme conditions than any other forms of life. They must be able to survive the stress of being first covered by water at high tide, then left uncovered and exposed to the air when the tide retreats a few hours later. They must also be able to survive the extremes of high and low temperature, salinity, and light that accompany such tidal changes.

Mobile species are able to limit their exposure to these extremes by moving in and out with the tides, either drifting on the current or swimming under their own power, but there are many less mobile or completely sessile estuarine plants and animals that can only sit and wait for whatever the next tide may bring them. Some are able to feed or reproduce only when submerged, which sharply limits their opportunities for both essential activities. That they are able to do this and survive, even thrive, must surely make them among the strongest, most sturdy forms of life on earth.

Despite these rigorous requirements for survival, a remarkably rich and diverse variety of flora and fauna has evolved within the estuaries. Most of these plants and animals are of marine origin and have adapted to the special conditions of the estuaries. During the ages they have spent getting used to this peculiar lifestyle, most species have found a niche or level where they feel most comfortable—places where bottom type, salinity, length of exposure to water or air, current strength, temperature, and wave action are to their liking—and in these places they

Barnacles appear in steadily increasing numbers . . . wherever there are rocks or snags to which they can attach themselves.

have established their colonies and gone about the business of reproduction and survival. Because of this habitat selectivity, life within estuaries tends to be vertically layered, with each species locating at a certain level of the tidal range. Some of these layers are sharply defined and others overlap so that the difference between them is not readily apparent to a casual observer, but knowledge of the zonal preferences of estuarine species is nevertheless always a useful tool in searching for and identifying them.

Horizontal layering also occurs, a result of fresh water flowing into the estuary. Since most estuarine species are of marine origin, they thrive best in areas of higher salinity and tend to shy away from river channels where the water is mostly or completely fresh. This is true, at least, for animals that dwell in the water itself or on the bottom surface. But where the bottom material consists of mud or sandy clay, it seems to offer protection against rapid changes in salinity; so long as the bottom is washed daily by the tide, the salinity of the saturated clay or mud bottom remains unchanged by the fresh water flowing over it at low tide. This allows burrowing creatures that prefer high levels of salinity to thrive even in mudflats frequently inundated by fresh water.

Life in estuaries also varies seasonally. The presence or absence of some mobile species—especially birds and fish—may be due to seasonal migrations, but populations of less mobile creatures usually fluctuate in response to the health of the local food chain. Not surprisingly, the phytoplankton that forms the base of the estuarine food chain is most abundant during summer months, generally from June to September, and estuarine biological activity reaches its peak during those months. The process that drives this explosion of life is linked closely to the spring runoff, which not only brings a fresh supply of nutrients but also assists in mixing the water column within the estuary, helping assure a maximum concentration of nutrients from both fresh and salt water. The longer days of late spring and early summer, with their increased light intensity and warmer temperatures, help accelerate phytoplankton growth.

A comprehensive description of all the diverse forms of estuarine life is beyond the scope of this book, but there is obvious value in describing those species most visible or important to estuary anglers. Even this could be a lengthy and formidable task without narrowing the focus to a particular area, so that is what I have done. Since Northwest estuaries are the primary focus of this book, the choice was easy and obvious: The habitat and life forms described are those of a typical or "generic" small, sheltered Pacific Northwest estuary. Estuaries at other latitudes may be expected to have somewhat different habitats and different forms of life, but the principal of vertical layering will always remain valid.

The stable, submerged surfaces of pilings support a veritable jungle of aquatic life.

Except for gamefish or important forage species, I have chosen to omit taxonomic names from this description; however, these names may be obtained by consulting references listed in the bibliography.

The Low-tide Zone

Only on a few days each year does the tide ebb far enough to expose the lowest layers of the estuary, but these tides of zero or minus range reveal many secrets hidden throughout the remainder of the year. They disclose the true character of the estuary, uncovering unsuspected channels or sandbars that influence currents and circulation at higher tide, and they expose sprawling colonies of life that are invisible at other times.

The lower tidal zone is a garden of plant life, and of all the plants that dwell in it the most important to anglers are the colonies of eelgrass with their long, waving, slender fronds. These colonies ordinarily are found in the deepest channels, growing from soft mud or clean sandy bottoms. The thick, tangled roots of the eelgrass plant firmly anchor the bottom material and provide a stable habitat for many small animals, including some that are important food for fish. The slim tendrils of these plants also offer shelter to fish and other creatures, and telegraph the movement of the tide. While the tide is ebbing, the eelgrass obediently bends and gently waves in the direction of the outward flow; but when the tide reverses, the eelgrass bends and waves in the opposite direction, and often this is the first visible evidence of the changing of the tide.

Rocks and rivulets uncovered by the tide.

Eelgrass reaches its maximum growth and abundance during the warm spring and summer months, retreating—but never disappearing—in the colder seasons of autumn and winter; the same is true for many of the creatures that live in, around, or under eelgrass colonies. Many links of the estuarial food chain are present in the eelgrass community, beginning with the microscopic bacteria and diatoms that grow upon its leaves and give them their characteristic olive-brown color.

The leaves also host small snails, jellyfish, sea slugs, anemones, and clams, and give shelter to sea stars (starfish), Dungeness and red crabs. Yet of all the organisms that live in this community as both predator and prey, the most important to anglers are the flatworms, ribbonworms, and crustacea—the broken-back and grass shrimp; isopods (pillbugs) and amphipods (scuds)—that are avidly

sought by estuarine fish and readily imitated by anglers. The presence of these animals makes eelgrass beds attractive places to fish on any tide, but the location and extent of the beds usually is apparent only on the lowest tides.

Preferring the same type of bottom, and often mistaken for eelgrass, is the surfgrass plant, which also has long, waving, slender leaves but is true green in color and lacks the tangled, matted root structure of eelgrass. As a shelter and food source, however, surfgrass is nearly as appealing to fish—and anglers—as the eelgrass beds.

In recent years, spartina grass—commonly called smooth cordgrass—has invaded the low-tide zones of many Northwest estuaries. This non-native plant, brought in around the turn of the century for use as packing material around shipments of oysters, forms dense colonies that become sediment traps, causing previously productive habitat areas to fill in and accelerating the estuary's aging process so it evolves more quickly into a marsh or meadow. Spartina has become a serious threat to rearing areas for juvenile salmonids, marine fish, Dungeness crab, oysters, shorebirds, waterfowl, and many other valuable species, and chemical or mechanical means have been employed in an effort to control it in some areas. Washington's Willapa Bay is an example; there, commercial oyster growers have begun chemical spraying to keep spartina grass from destroying oyster habitat. Despite such efforts, it appears likely spartina will remain a common—and unfortunate—feature of many Northwest estuaries.

Rocky areas in the low-tide zone are home to many types of algae and kelp, colorful sponges, sea anemones, urchins, and sea squirts. This also is the habitat of many sea stars, with their multi-colored, multi-armed forms sprawled like beautiful ornaments across the bottom. There are also sea cucumbers, looking like giant colored pickles; chitons, wearing their segmented shells like armored plate; snails with spiral shells, and limpets that look like little coolie hats. There are vivid sea slugs and a variety of crabs, including hermit, kelp, and red crabs. Broken-back shrimp lie hidden in the algae of the tidal pools, often matching themselves to the colors of the algae, and under rocks blenny eels and flathead clingfish will be found. Rocky areas of the low-tide zone also are habitat for the small and now rare native Olympic oyster.

Where the bottom is sandy it is often cluttered with large colonies of sand dollars, with their slate-gray or purplish flat-cone shapes, and occasionally the large, twisted shell of a great moon snail may be seen. Black-tailed shrimp and scallops are common sandflat burrowers, and on the surface of the flats, isopods and amphipods graze on decaying plant and animal remains.

The basket cockle reaches its greatest numbers in this habitat and its empty shells, along with those of littleneck clams, are often visible on the bottom, evidence of thriving buried colonies. Occasionally there is the startling sight of a sand sole breaking free of concealment on the bottom, or the quick movement of a ubiquitous staghorn sculpin that is all too willing to grab an angler's fly in its enormous mouth.

Muddy bottoms in the low-tide zone are home to sea pens, burrowing worms, ghost shrimp, and blue mud shrimp, as well as horse mussels and several types of clams. Isopods and amphipods are common here, too, especially the scud-like amphipod *Anisogammarus*, a favorite food of sea-run cutthroat. Skates and flounder are often seen, and little arrow, bay, or black-eyed goby cruise about on mudflats dotted with the burrows of ghost shrimp. Huge colonies of Japanese oysters are found here, as they are on all types of bottom all the way up through the mid-tide zone. All these things, and more, become visible when the tide withdraws far enough to reveal them.

The Mid-tide Zone

In the tidal range from zero to about nine feet in most Pacific Northwest estuaries, the variety of life is nearly as bewildering as it is in the low-tide zone, and many of the same forms are represented. But the careful observer will note gradual changes.

Rocky bottoms at this level are commonly inhabited by sea stars, snails, limpets, black chitons, and anemones, along with hermit crabs, tiny porcelain crabs, and others. There is a wide variety of algae (seaweed) and many small crustaceans, pillbugs, amphipods, and worms. The olive-brown pillbug *Idotea wosnesenskii*, which may grow more than an inch long, is especially numerous and is another important food source for sea-run cutthroat trout.

Mussels, with their characteristic blue-black sharply oval shells, cluster around rocks or old wood, and rock cockles—more popularly known as littleneck clams—are common. Barnacles also are more numerous, appearing in steadily increasing numbers the closer one gets to the top of the tidal range, wherever there are rocks or snags to which they can attach themselves.

The organically rich mud and sandflats of the mid-tide zone are home to an exceedingly diverse array of life, mostly creatures that burrow into the mud to escape the lack of surface cover. When uncovered by the tide, the mudflats come alive with miniature geysers, the spurts of buried clams and cockles, and reveal the burrows of ghost and mud shrimp. Algae patches host slime-trailing ribbon worms and free-swimming or crawling polychaete worms, tiny brittle stars and pillbugs, amphipods, shrimps, and crabs. Most visible of all are the oysters, the large, often cultivated Japanese oysters racked up in incredible jumbled rows of sharp-edged shells gleaming whitely in the sun. As we shall see later, these oyster beds—sometimes incredibly vast—hold a special attraction for certain species of fish.

The High-tide Zone

Above the nine-foot mark to as high as the tide can reach there is a sharp change in the type and variety of life. Here dwell the creatures that are most exposed to the drying sun and air, covered by water only a short time each day, sometimes not covered for a days at a time except by wind-driven spray, the splash of rain or the wet wash of fog. Along cobbled beaches, the most obvious animals are barnacles, limpets, and snails, such as the Sitka periwinkle, plus the ubiquitous pillbugs and amphipods, taking shelter in crevices between rocks or cracks in the driftwood left stranded by the tide.

The little pillbugs *Gnorimosphaeroma oregonensis* and *luteum* are usually present in great numbers, and these also help form the diet of sea-run cutthroat trout. Purple shore crabs, small hermit crabs, ribbon worms, and mussels also are common in this environment.

Where the bottom is mostly mud, the fauna is dominated by mud-flat crabs, clams, snails, worms, and dense populations of the scud-like amphipod *Orchestia traskiana*. The isopod *Idotea wosnesenskii*, common among rocky areas of the mid-tide zone, is even more numerous at the high-tide level, and in this habitat it is sometimes called the rockweed pillbug. Like many amphipods and isopods, *Orchestia* and *Idotea* are primarily nocturnal in their habits, a fact of importance to anglers.

Stiff, spiky patches of saltwort may be found at the high-tide margins of many shallow bays and estuaries. This plant, also known as the pickleweed, is a relative of the prairie tumbleweed, and its colonies often mark the transition zone between marine and terrestrial habitat. Algae swept in by the tide often forms in mats around the roots of saltwort, and a tangled parasitic growth known as the saltmarsh dodder makes its home among the saltwort's stems. These thriving plant communities, usually covered by only the highest tides, provide shelter and food for snails, crabs, amphipods, and pillbugs, and the presence of all these animals makes saltwort colonies equally attractive to certain species of fish that follow the tide and feed along its edge.

Floating Docks and Pilings

Man-made structures provide fertile habitats for life forms that differ in many respects from those found along the slopes of the estuary floor. Anchored wooden floats are

The mouth of Tenmile Creek, a typical small Oregon coastal estuary.

designed to rise and fall freely with the tide while their lower surfaces always remain submerged or in contact with the water. Pilings, on the other hand, often are sunk in dredged or deeper areas so the tide may rise and fall along their upper lengths while their lower portions always remain submerged. The stable, submerged surfaces of these structures support a veritable jungle of aquatic life (although it may be a long while before life begins to colonize a chemically treated piling after it is sunk in place).

Seaweeds, sponges, jellyfish, sea anemones, sea stars, sea cucumbers, urchins, barnacles, chitons, and limpets are all common forms of life on floats and pilings. Mussels and jingle-shell oysters also attach themselves tenaciously to wooden surfaces, and porcelain crabs occupy the crevices. Hydroids—invertebrate animals that look like plants—also cling to floats and startle their unsuspecting prey with stinging cells, while diatoms, sea spiders, sea slugs, amphipods, and flatworms live among their streaming branches and trailers. Tube-building polychaete worms find residence here along with free-swimming scaleworms.

Little broken-back shrimp cling to the seaweed growing on floats and pilings. These shrimp, which grow scarcely more than an inch in length, are characterized by a sharp bend in their third abdominal segment, hence their name—although they might just as easily be called humpback shrimp. Usually green, olive, or reddish brown in color, and slightly translucent, they swim backward and provide a ready source of food for fish.

Coon-stripe shrimp, distinctive for their vivid brown, red, or white markings, also are often found around floats. Members of the commercially important genus *Pandalus*, they grow to several inches in length, but are often taken by fish in smaller sizes.

Floats and pilings also provide friendly habitat for the usual hosts of copepods, amphipods, and pillbugs. Among the latter is the previously mentioned *Idotea wosnesenskii*, which may grow to a length of 1 1/2 inches and varies in color from bright green to brown or nearly black. It clings to seaweed on docks or pilings. Also common here, especially in low-saline estuarine environments, is the fat little gray Oregon pillbug, *Gnorimosphaeroma oregonensis*, another seaweed lover that rarely exceeds a half-inch in length but is taken in great numbers by sea-run trout.

At the lower ends of pilings—those portions usually submerged, even at low tide—are more anemones, more hydroid colonies, more seaweed and kelp, stalked truncates and slabs of red, yellow or brown "sea pork," sea stars, sea cucumbers, sea urchins and kelp crabs. The tiny isopod known as the "gribble" also is present in great numbers, busily burrowing into the surfaces of pilings and making meals of the wood, the aquatic equivalent of the termite. Over time these animals may riddle a shaft of wood, but even more damage may be done by the Pacific Coast shipworm—actually a bivalve mollusk—that burrows even more deeply into the wood. Fortunately, the Pacific Coast shipworm, a relative of the notorious teredo, tends to avoid less saline waters.

The abundance of life around pilings or under floats is itself enough to make them attractive places for fish. The pile perch, for example, gets its name from its habit of dining on the readily available food it finds among old pilings. But floats and docks also are worth fishing because of the shade and shelter they provide, especially on bright days.

Converging estuaries: Smith Creek on the left, the North River in the foreground, with Willapa Bay in the distance.

The Fish Life of Estuaries

A few fish common in estuaries already have been mentioned, and later we shall deal at length with the gamefish that are most frequent targets for estuary anglers. But there are many other species of fish that spend all or part of their lives in estuaries, including some that are important as forage fish, and some that are interesting simply because they are often seen by anglers fishing in the estuaries.

Among the most common forage-fish species in Northwest waters are Pacific herring *(Clupea harengus)*, which also are fished commercially and are widely used as bait by salmon fishermen; the eulachon or candlefish *(Thaleichthys pacificus)*; the three-spined stickleback *(Gasterosteus aculeatus)*, which is important during seasonal migrations; and the Pacific sand lance *(Ammodytes hexapterus)*, a small, snake-like, beach-spawning fish present during summer and early fall. All are inviting subjects for imitation by fly fishers. At least five species of sculpin also are common and some fly tiers also have made efforts to imitate them, although they are more important as forage fish in Oregon and California estuaries than they are farther north.

One of the most visible—and ugly—estuarine fish is the spiny dogfish *(Squalus acanthias)*, a shark often seen prowling the sandflats. Although specimens more than four feet in length are rare and the dogfish's only menace to humans is a stinging dorsal spine, it is a nuisance to both sport and commercial fishermen (it steals bait and its sandpaper-like skin damages nets). Dogfish will take a fly, but why anyone would want to fish for them is a good question.

Other species likely to be present at times in the estuaries include the Northern anchovy *(Engraulis mordax)*; the Pacific sardine *(Sardinops sagax)*, surf smelt *(Hypomesus pretiosus)*, longfin smelt *(Spirinchus thaleichthys)*, saddleback gunnel *(Pholis ornata)*, kelp greenling *(Hexagrammos decagrammus)*, masked greenling *(Hexagrammos octogrammus)*, ling cod *(Ophiodon elongatus)*, speckled sanddab *(Citharichthys stigmaeus)*, English sole *(Parophrys vetulus)*, sand sole *(Psettichthys melanosticus)*, starry flounder *(Platichthys stellatus)*, various species of rockfish *(Sebastes)*, and various sea perch (family

Embiotocidae). Of these, the anchovy, sardine, and smelt are sometimes important as forage fish, particularly the anchovy, and many of the others—most especially the sea perch, rockfish, starry flounder, and ling cod—may be taken on the fly. More about them later.

Estuarine Mammals

Several types of mammals are found in estuaries, and while they have little importance to anglers—except that they may temporarily disrupt the fishing—they often provide spectacular sights, and they are an important part of the estuarine food chain.

The most common mammal of Northwest estuaries is the harbor seal. This cautious but friendly animal often may be seen lounging on a float in the noonday sun, or popping its head above the surface for a curious look at a fisherman. But while seals are smart, playful, and fun to watch, they can seriously disturb the fishing. They feed primarily on bottom fish, but also may attack more active fish such as salmon or trout, and whenever a seal is in the area the fish will run for cover.

Other mammals are less common, but occasionally an angler may see a harbor porpoise, river otter, or California sea lion. Much more spectacular is a chance encounter with a pod of killer whales, although these rarely seem to enter confined estuaries. More often they are seen at a distance— great, graceful, black-and-white animals with dorsals like triangular black flags, rolling cleanly through the waves almost as if they were traveling in slow motion. They have a legendary ability to put all fish to flight in any area they are traveling through, and salmon are among their favorite food.

Some years ago in a well-publicized incident in the Strait of Juan de Fuca, an angler hooked and was playing a salmon that was taken by a killer whale. The angler suddenly found himself fast to the whale until his reel seized up in a cloud of smoke and the line broke.

Killer whales also are intelligent and friendly creatures, but their size makes it unwise to go near them in small boats. For that matter, federal law prohibits the harassment of any marine mammal, and the definition of harassment includes approaching them closely in a boat.

The Waterfowl and Bird Life of Estuaries

The combination of water, marsh, and wetlands in and around estuaries makes them ideal places for migrating waterfowl, fish-eating waterbirds, shorebirds, and terrestrial birds. Indeed, the bird life of estuaries is bewildering in abundance and variety, and most of it is highly visible.

Among the waterfowl, canvasback ducks, greater and lesser scaup, American wigeon, bufflehead, and eelgrass-eating black brant are most commonly seen in the winter months. The numbers of all these species increase in March and April, when pintail ducks become abundant too. But during and after the breeding season and the northward migration in May, June, and July, the estuaries are mostly empty of waterfowl. Either they have gone, or they remain out of sight in their nesting areas, shielded by the thick vegetation of the salt marshes or isolated on spits and islands. Mallards, pintails, and migrating black brant are the species most often seen during these months.

The greatest migrations occur in the fall, beginning as early as late August with the pintail and American wigeon.

Of all the fishermen I know, the great blue heron is the best.

Mallards and green-winged teal also are often seen at this time. Canvasbacks, scaup, and bufflehead arrive again in October, and the haunting call of the majestic Canada goose is heard from on high in October and November, although relatively few of these great birds pause to rest in the estuaries.

The noisy coot is present during the winter, from November through March, and winter also is the time when one is most likely to see such other species as the common goldeneye, scoter, ruddy duck, and merganser.

Western and red-necked grebes paddle and bob about the estuaries from October until April, and the high, ululating call of the common loon is heard occasionally through the morning fog from April to July and sometimes in other seasons. Other fish-eating waterbirds that frequent the estuaries include cormorants, whose numbers have increased very rapidly in recent years, the common murre, the rare marbled murrelet, and the odd rhinoceros auklet.

Of all the fishermen I know, the great blue heron is the best. Standing stock-still on long, spindly legs, it is the very epitome of patience, and its slate-gray color blends perfectly with the pastel shades of the estuary. Despite its motionless visage, the heron is ever wary and alert, and its patience is rewarded whenever a small, unsuspecting fish ventures within range of its long neck and great straight beak. Almost impossible to approach closely, the heron will lift off with great slow-motion wingbeats, and its loud, hoarse, squawking cry is a familiar sound as it flies low across the estuaries. The heron's numbers have increased rapidly since persistent pesticides, such as DDT, were banned from use, and heron are present in the estuaries every month of the year, although they are perhaps most commonly seen from July through December.

The belted kingfisher is a far less patient angler than the heron, always fidgety, nervous, and noisy. It favors trees along the shoreline, especially those with limbs extending over the water, and when it can sit still on one of these long enough to see a small fish swimming down below, it plummets like a colorful missile through the surface to capture its prey, then rises again in a flurry of wings and spray with the unfortunate victim squirming in its beak. While the heron simply moves on without complaint whenever a human angler approaches too closely, the kingfisher responds with raucous chatter whenever a fisherman invades its territory. Yet the kingfisher's nervous nature always makes it fun to watch.

There are always gulls in the estuaries, wheeling gracefully on extended wings through invisible currents of air or swarming to pick at the rotting salmon carcasses near the mouth of a stream. Their lonely call is the most consistent music of the estuaries, and never have I spent a day of estuary fishing when it was absent.

Different seasons bring different species and numbers of gulls. They are most common from March to September, when they congregate about their nesting sites, and least numerous from October through February, although always still present. Glaucous-winged and mew gulls and black-legged kittiwakes are most common from December until March, with Western gulls also becoming abundant in the latter month. From April until June, Western and glaucous-winged gull populations reach their peak, and Bonaparte, California, and ringbilled gulls also may be seen. Heerman's gulls come later in the summer and by September are gone again. The graceful tern, a relative of the gulls, is a common estuary visitor from April to June and again in the fall.

Like the gulls, Northwestern crows may be seen picking over the remains of spawned-out salmon at the creek-mouths in the fall, or scavenging the beaches along the high-tide line for whatever they can find to eat at any time.

Far more noble and majestic are the fish-eating ospreys or seahawks, which usually appear in April and stay until fall, and the bald eagles, which remain throughout the year.

Shorebirds are the most numerous of all, dominated by the Dunlin and Western sandpipers, which are present in great numbers through the winter, running along the tide-flats or rising in tight formations to perform their amazing synchronized turns. Other shorebirds begin arriving from the south in April and their migration peaks in mid-May with more sandpipers moving in, followed by red knots and Dowitchers. June is a slack month, but in July sand-pipers, Dowitchers, least sandpipers, black-bellied plovers, and ruddy turnstones are numerous. Their populations peak in August before they start returning to the south, with their fall migration reaching its height in October.

Other species often seen in the estuaries include the killdeer, snipe, long-billed curlew, whimbrel, greater and lesser yellowlegs, and sanderling, plus still others seen only rarely.

The marshes and wetlands around the estuary are visited by many terrestrial species, especially during summer. The majestic marsh hawk flies low over the salt marshes in the summer twilight, and great horned owls, red-tailed hawks, rare peregrine falcons, Cooper's hawks, and other raptors also frequent the marshes and wetlands, hunting smaller shorebirds and small mammals.

A gull hunkers down on a breezy winter day on Puget Sound.

Estuarine Insect Life

Insects, too, play a role in the ecological web of estuaries, albeit a small one. Saltwater insects are few, but they are of some interest, and terrestrial insects are sometimes carried onto estuarine waters just as they are to inland lakes and streams. Of these we will see more later.

Red Tide and Bioluminescence

Red tide and bioluminescence are two other phenomena common to Pacific Northwest estuaries. The first is caused by a reproductive pulse or "bloom" of free-floating microscopic plants called dinoflagellates, part of the phytoplankton, and usually occurs after a spell of warm summer weather. Its name is derived from the great patches of reddish-brown water formed by the countless millions of tiny floating plants; these typically appear along tidelines in estuaries.

In moderation, red-tide blooms can be beneficial; the microscopic plants provide both oxygen and food for other creatures. However, the dinoflagellates that create red tides also contain a toxin that can cause paralytic shellfish poisoning in humans; this toxin has no effect on clams, oysters or mussels that consume the tiny plants, but it can have devastating effects on humans who eat the shellfish. Red-tide blooms are especially large and common in estuaries polluted by the discharge of raw or treated sewage, of which unfortunately there are many in the Northwest, and they often lead to emergency closures of shellfish harvesting during summer months.

Bioluminescence is the beautiful and ghostly ephemeral light that appears when estuarine waters are disturbed on a dark night. It is actually caused by the same dinoflagellates that form red tides, but in this case their role is entirely benign. Each microscopic plant responds with a bright, rapid flash of light, usually lasting less than a tenth of a second, whenever there is a nearby disturbance in its environment. Often the wake of a motorboat traveling at night will leave a trail of luminescence; slapping the water with an oar or banging the side of an aluminum boat to produce a loud noise also will stimulate a brief local explosion of luminescence.

The flash emitted by these plants is a "cold" light, lacking the heat that is a byproduct of most chemical reactions. It is believed to be some sort of alarm or defense mechanism, but its biological purpose is not fully understood. Bioluminescence in the estuaries is most spectacular during summer months when dinoflagellate populations are highest, but it is a year-round phenomenon, apparent even in winter, providing evidence that the water is always full of life even though not all of it can be seen by a human eye.

Cape Creek meets the Pacific Ocean, another small estuary on the Oregon coast.

Estuarine Ecology

The shape of the estuary, its tidal range, the rivers flowing into it, the circulation pattern within it, and all its aquatic plants, animals, fish, and birds are tied together in an ecosystem so complex it almost defies human understanding. Through countless ages of selection, experiment, and change, the pattern of estuarine life has evolved with each element in its own vital niche, dependent upon all the others even as they are dependent upon it.

The estuary's shape, tidal range, freshwater inflow, and circulation determine the distribution and deposition of the nutrients contributed by land and sea, and all those factors—plus the tidal range, current, and bottom type—determine the distribution and relative abundance of aquatic plants and animals. These plants and animals in turn determine the abundance and distribution of fish, mammals, and birds—the highest links, other than humans, in the complex estuarial food chain.

Once or twice each day the tide rushes into the salt marsh at the rim of the estuary and leaves a tiny portion of its vast cargo of salts and minerals, then withdraws; the sun warms the fertile soil, and around the saltwort stems and beneath the mats of algae vast populations of pillbugs, amphipods, snails, and crabs breed and grow and prosper and die. Bacteria attack the victims and the dead algae that shelters them, and the process of decay begins; the high tide returns and carries the decaying remnants into the outer estuary, where amphipods and other creatures join the feast. Some of these end up in turn as food for fish or foraging shorebirds; some of the fish in turn become meals for kingfishers, herons or seals; and some of the shorebirds may become a raptor's dinner. At every step, the number of consumers is smaller but their size and appetites are larger. At length, with the eventual death of the kingfisher, heron, seal, or raptor, decay and scavenging begin anew, and their bodies too are recycled and returned to the strict economy of the estuary.

Meanwhile, the migratory fish, birds, and mammals that use the estuary only temporarily for rest or for food carry some of its organic wealth with them on their journeys, ultimately feeding other natural systems when their own flesh eventually is recycled back to the water or the land.

At every level of the tide, in every type of habitat, popu-

lations of animals and plants breed and expand to the limits of the carrying capacity of the environment. This is natural law: A habitat will support the greatest variety of species and individual numbers possible within its carrying capacity, but no more. It is a law that humans have been slow to learn, assuming, as they invariably do, that altering the estuarine habitat by "development," pollution, filling, or other measures means only that the plants and animals living there can relocate somewhere else. The truth is that every natural habitat already is fully occupied, and the destruction of an estuary or any part of it inevitably means the destruction of all the creatures that live within it.

At the very top of the food chain are humans, who have been given dominion over the earth and all other living things. But their position at the apex also means that humans must depend more than any other creature on the health of the ecosystem that supports them. This is something else humans have been slow to learn, and the evidence is plain in their careless treatment of estuaries, which—as we have seen—are the richest producers of life on the planet.

Still, humans may enter the estuaries as individuals in harmony with their surroundings, synchronizing their behavior with all the teeming life of the estuary. No less than the eagle, the heron, or the seal, a human angler is entitled to keep some of the fish that come to him; unlike them, however, he or she may make a conscious choice to return them to the water if there is no need for them other than for the sport they give. By so doing, humans can use the wealth of the estuary without using it up, and take their pleasure from it without subtracting from its abundance of life.

That abundance is apparent in the foregoing description of estuarine life. Yet it is a description that is by no means complete, even for the typical small, sheltered Pacific Northwest estuary I have chosen as an example. The species, abundance, habits, and distribution of plants and animals may be different in the estuaries of other locales, but usually they will be no less complex or varied. This example is meant to show the wealth and complexity of life in only a single estuarine habitat—and perhaps now it is clear why it was necessary to limit the choice to only one. Let the example serve as a guide to those who live on other shores, for they will find equal wealth wherever tides and rivers meet.

A dead, spawned-out chum salmon in the shallows off the mouth of Little Mission Creek, Hood Canal, Washington.

III
PACIFIC SALMON IN NORTHWEST ESTUARIES

It was salmon that first brought people to the estuaries. The Indians who were the original inhabitants of the Pacific Northwest lived mainly along rivers or estuaries and depended heavily on salmon for their livelihood. Even today, salmon still draw people to the estuaries, with great numbers of sport and commercial fishermen contending for ever-diminishing runs.

The five North American species of Pacific salmon, along with the steelhead, the cutthroat, and the Dolly Varden char, are all anadromous fish, meaning they hatch in fresh water but migrate to sea at some point in their lives, eventually returning to fresh water to spawn. But there the commonality ends, for these fish display an amazing variety of life histories and degrees of anadromy. Salmon are the most highly anadromous and most valuable commercial species, and they have received the most attention from fisheries researchers, so a great deal is known about them and their life histories and habits. Historically, they also have captured the attention of the largest number of anglers.

Of the five species native to North American waters, four of them— the coho, chum, pink, and chinook—provide significant estuary fisheries for fly anglers. Only the sockeye fails to make the list of fly-rod fish, but that omission may be temporary; after all, it has not been many years since conventional wisdom held that none of the Pacific salmon could be taken on a fly. Then it was discovered that both chinook and coho, especially the latter, could be made to respond consistently to flies; more recently, enterprising anglers have found ways to capture chums and pinks. Now we know that under the right conditions, and with the right fly patterns and techniques, these four species are far more responsive to flies than previous generations of anglers ever dreamed. Perhaps, in the near future, someone will figure out the secrets of taking sockeye on the fly.

Coho (Silver) Salmon

The coho salmon, *Oncorhynchus kisutch*, undoubtedly is the most important species to estuary anglers, not only because it is perhaps the most willing fly-rod fish but also because it is accessible to anglers at more stages in its life than any of the others. It is the most trout-like of all the Pacific salmon; a healthy, well-conditioned, sea-run coho is the quintessential picture of a gamefish, streamlined and silver and full of energy and strength from its long feeding journey across the North Pacific. Historically, coho ran to Northwest rivers in great numbers, and their characteristic spectacular leaps and high-speed runs have long made them great favorites of sport fishermen.

Most sport fishing for cohos is for returning adults, but in some locations they are also available to estuary anglers as feisty, light-tackle opponents in their pre-migratory stage, or as adult "resident" fish. This availability at different stages of its life cycle has contributed substantially to the coho's popularity as a sport fish.

The coho typically spawns in small, low-gradient streams that drain directly into salt water or flow as tributaries into larger rivers, although some coho ascend all the way to the headwaters of rivers to spawn. In all these preferences they are similar to cutthroat trout. Spawning takes place from late October through January, and the actual spawning ritual is similar to that of most salmonids. As is true of all the North American species of Pacific salmon, coho die after spawning.

The incubation period of coho salmon eggs varies with temperature, ranging from as little as six weeks in warmer southern streams to as long as 14 weeks in colder northern rivers. In streams occupied by both coho and cutthroat, the coho fry usually emerge earlier than the cutthroat, giving them a competitive advantage. Throughout the southern part of their range, which extends as far south as Monterey Bay, California, most coho fry remain in their native streams at least a year before they reach smolting stage, but two years of stream residence is not unusual for fry hatched in colder northern rivers.

Smolting, when it does occur, takes place in the spring—anytime from April in the south until early June in the north,

A bright resident coho taken on the fly in Puget Sound. It was released moments after the photo was taken.

usually peaking about the middle of May—and once they enter the estuaries, most coho set out immediately on their ocean feeding migration. However, in Puget Sound and in some of the sheltered sounds and bays of the Inside Passage, a small percentage of each class of coho smolts remains behind and "residualizes," never leaving for the open sea. These fish feed on phytoplankton, fish larvae, and amphipods until they reach a size large enough to begin preying on small forage fish. They are often found in shallow water along cobbled, rocky beaches, where they may sometimes be taken easily on flies, but they are sensitive to light and on bright days frequently head for deeper or more open waters. This brings them in contact with another important food source, the euphasid shrimp, usually found only in deeper water. These resident coho often travel in schools, like cutthroat, and the two species may sometimes be found intermingled in the estuaries.

It has been estimated that only three to five percent of each coho year class residualizes in Puget Sound and the percentage for other areas is probably similar. The figures seem small, but since the number of outmigrating smolts is usually large the actual number of fish that remain behind to residualize may be sizable, and these young "feeder" coho provide an important sport fishery. A wild resident coho that smolted and left its native stream in the spring may enter the sport catch as early as December of the same year, by which time it usually has grown to a length of 10 or 12 inches. Under favorable conditions, it may continue growing as much as two inches a month, so by the following May—after a year in salt water—it measures 18 to 20 inches and is a very worthy opponent on a light fly rod.

After spending their first year feeding along the beaches, Puget Sound resident coho typically begin a "mini migration" north into the Strait of Juan de Fuca, where they continue feeding and growing throughout their second summer. Then, in the fall, after about 16 months in salt water, they join their returning sea-run brethren and head back for their rivers of origin in southern Puget Sound—or, in the case of hatchery fish, back to their release points. En route they pass the western shore of Whidbey Island, or Point No Point at the northern tip of the Kitsap Peninsula, and from these locations they are sometimes taken by fly casters working from the beaches. By mid-October, when the survivors have reached south Puget Sound, most average three to five pounds in weight, a few even more, and in the relatively brief time before they begin to color up for spawning, they provide superlative fly-rod angling opportunities.

Researchers discovered more than 20 years ago that if hatchery-reared coho were held past the time they would normally smolt, most would residualize when they were finally released in Puget Sound, so they began intentionally delaying the release of some fish to provide more year-round sport fishing for cohos in the Sound. Now the Washington State Department of Fish and Wildlife operates an extensive delayed-release program to augment the natural population of Puget Sound resident coho. The program has had its ups and downs, but on the whole has been quite successful, and hatchery-reared fish have contributed very substantially to the sport fishery.

Some of the other naturally occurring resident coho populations north of Puget Sound provide local sport fisheries, but none is as extensive or as well known as the Puget Sound fishery. Farther south, where large, sheltered sounds

Not all estuaries are wild, unspoiled places. Here the author fishes Sinclair Inlet, with the Navy's mothball fleet at the Puget Sound Naval Shipyard in the background.

and estuaries are rare or lacking altogether, there are no resident coho fisheries.

But while resident coho are significant in Puget Sound, the most important coho salmon fishery in Puget Sound and elsewhere involves returning sea-run adults. Obeying the instincts coded in their genes, these fish turn back from their high-seas feeding migration in early summer and start heading south along the coasts of Alaska and British Columbia. They continue feeding as they travel south, and as each separate stock nears its home river it peels off to enter the estuary where that river meets the sea. By August this mighty southward-moving wave of fish bursts into the narrow waters between Vancouver Island and the British Columbia mainland, and by Labor Day it has split into two spearheads, one moving eastward into the Strait of Juan de Fuca to return to the rivers draining into Puget Sound, the other continuing south along the Washington coast to the Columbia River and its tributaries or to the Oregon and California coastal streams that lie beyond.

This great migration is truly one of the wonders of nature, but the returning coho must run a long and dangerous gantlet to reach their home rivers. They are subject to intensive commercial fisheries almost every inch of the way, and their numbers inevitably are sharply reduced by the relentless, ever-present parade of nets. During most of their journey through the Inside Passage they are also available to sport anglers, but it is not until they reach constricted waters near Vancouver Island that they are subjected to a really intensive sport fishery. From that point onward, however, they are sought as avidly by sport anglers as by commercial fishermen, and when the survivors finally enter the estuaries of their native rivers, their numbers are only a small fraction of all that began the long return. Estuary anglers must be content with what remains.

Sometimes that is more than enough. By late September or early October, when returning coho adults begin entering the inner estuaries throughout the southern part of their range, they will have spent more than two years feeding at sea. Most will weigh between six and twelve pounds, though some will be even larger, and they will be at the very peak of their form—thick and firm in the body, with bright silver flanks and backs the color of the deep blue sea, as handsome as a fish can ever be. They also are as strong as they will ever be, and they form in schools whose presence is revealed by the sight of porpoising, rolling, leaping fish. The sight of such a school is sure to produce a strong flow of adrenaline in every fisherman.

Depending on water conditions in their home river, the cohos may remain in the estuary a week or two, awaiting the right combination of river level and tide to start them on their upstream journey. During that time most remain in good condition, but very soon their silver flanks will begin fading to a burnished bronze, a certain signal that spawning cannot be far off, and their gleaming perfection quickly dulls and becomes ever less attractive. At most, an estuary fly fisher has about a two-week window in which to find these fish at their best. Some fresh coho may continue entering the estuaries until the end of November, but usually the bulk of the run has come and gone by the middle or end of October.

The coho's preference for small, fragile spawning streams has exposed it to a wide range of environmental insults, including those known to fisheries managers as the "four H's"—hydroelectric dams, harvest impacts, hatcheries, and habitat destruction. Hydroelectric dams, such as those on the Columbia River, have mainly affected coho populations spawning in tributary streams; harvest by commercial and sport fisheries has reduced many runs below historic levels; and fish raised in hatcheries and released in the wild presumably have compromised the genetic integrity of many native populations. As for habitat destruction, activities such as logging, real-estate "development," diking and filling, water diversion, and pollution have combined to wipe out much of the spawning and rearing habitat that once existed throughout the natural range of the coho salmon.

Away from the crowd, a solitary angler battles a chum salmon on the beach of Hood Canal.

The homeward migration of the coho salmon also carries it through murky political waters, first those of the United States (in Alaska), then Canada, then into U.S. waters again, and this has added immeasurably to the problems of management. Commercial fishermen of one nation traditionally take many fish bound for rivers of the other, and the apparent inability of negotiators to agree on an equitable distribution of the catch, or the measures necessary for conservation, undoubtedly has contributed significantly to the decline of native runs.

Ocean conditions also are critical to coho survival, and recent changes in ocean currents and temperatures, as well as other possible factors not yet identified, have taken a further severe toll on these fish. So has increased predation;

protective measures conferred on marine mammals by federal legislation have resulted in rapid population increases among these animals, which feed on coho and other salmonids. The West Coast sea lion population, for example, increased from an estimated 36,000 in 1978 to 67,000 ten years later; in Oregon waters alone, the harbor seal population increased from an estimated 4,000-5000 in 1984 to 9,500-12,500 in 1992. The effect of these increases is evident in the incidence of scars noted on fish passing over Bonneville Dam. In 1980, less than 1 percent of the chinook salmon passing over Bonneville bore scars from attacks by marine mammals, but during the period 1990-1992, 40 to 50 percent of the migrating chinook had such scars. The incidence of scars on all salmonids passing over Bonneville in 1990 was 19 percent.

Sea-bird populations, especially cormorants and common murres, also have grown substantially since the use of DDT was banned, and this too has led to increased predation, especially on young salmon migrating outward through the estuaries. By itself, the increase in marine mammal and sea-bird predation may not necessarily be a cause of declining salmon populations, but it may prevent their recovery.

The cumulative effect of all these pressures has been a decline of wild coho runs to the point that some stocks in Oregon and Washington already are extinct, and many others have been proposed for endangered-species classification. The rapid decline of wild stocks has led to severe restrictions on both sport and commercial fisheries in Oregon and Washington during the past few years, and the future probably holds more such restrictions. Many other salmon and sea-run trout stocks have suffered from the same problems affecting coho, requiring imposition of similar restrictions.

The growing plight of salmon in general and coho in particular has focused more public attention on these fish than ever before, and that can only be for the good. But even with increasing public pressure to restore habitat and protect remaining runs, the future of the coho is uncertain at best. For the present, there is good fishing for resident populations in South Puget Sound and for ocean-run coho mostly in the protected bays and estuaries of the Inside Passage along the coasts of British Columbia and Southeast Alaska.

Chum (Dog) Salmon

The chum salmon, *Oncorhynchus keta*, is a relatively recent addition to the fly fisher's catalog of estuarine species.

This is due in large part to hatchery programs that have enhanced natural runs, bringing fish back in sufficient numbers to make a sport fishery possible. During the past decade, the success of these programs has made fly fishing for chums extremely popular in the estuaries of Hood Canal and South Puget Sound. It is less popular in areas without large-scale chum-enhancement programs, especially British Columbia, but there is some excellent fly fishing for chums in parts of Southeast Alaska where natural runs are still abundant.

Chum salmon spawn in streams of all sizes. A 1973 mapping program by the U.S. Geological Survey and the Bureau of Sport Fisheries and Wildlife (as it was known then) identified chum salmon spawning runs in 27 of 28 streams flowing into southern Hood Canal. These ranged from systems as large as the Skokomish River to creeks so small they barely warranted local names. But even in larger rivers like the Skokomish, adult chum usually do not run very far upstream to spawn, and their offspring migrate seaward immediately after emerging from the gravel.

Chum salmon may begin spawning as early as September in the northern part of their range, but most spawning activity takes place from mid-November through early January. As with the other North American species of Pacific salmon, the adults all die after spawning. Since they prefer streams of all sizes, chums inevitably spawn in many of the same streams used by cutthroat and coho, but because their offspring head downstream immediately after hatching there is little or no in-stream competition with these other species.

Young chum salmon may emerge from the gravel and start their downstream migration as early as February in some southern streams, but the peak migrations usually occur in April, ending by the middle of May. The downstream movement takes place so soon after emergence that many young chum still carry vestiges of their yolk sacs when they reach salt water. Usually they linger several days in the lower tidal reaches of their home stream, or in salt marshes near its mouth, or in the upper portion of its estuary, forming into schools and feeding on tiny copepods, amphipods, and other organisms found in eelgrass beds or in the shallows near the beach. The length of time they spend in the estuary apparently is closely related to the abundance of such food; if it is plentiful they will remain to take advantage of it, but if not they will head immediately for the open sea.

Chum that emerge late and enter salt water in April or early May when food is more plentiful tend to stay longer in the estuaries. These fish grow rapidly, feeding in the shallows, until they reach a length of about two inches; then they usually move into deeper water and begin their seaward migration. Their migratory route takes them northward into the Gulf of Alaska, where they may spend anywhere from three to five years feeding, although most will return at age four to spawn. Depending on the length of time they have spent at sea, returning adults may weigh anywhere from six to sixteen pounds, although much larger individuals have been caught.

Like coho, chums begin heading south from Alaskan waters early in the summer, with each separate stock turning away to enter its home estuary as the migrating schools proceed down the coast. Also like coho, chums may be subject to commercial fishing all along their route, but since they are not as commercially valuable as coho they are not targeted as intensively. That changes, however, when they near their home waters; there they are sought virtually around the clock by gillnetters and purse seiners in so-called "terminal fisheries."

The first adults returning to Hood Canal streams may arrive as early as September, although the great bulk of the run does not appear until early November. Fish returning to Puget Sound rivers may appear even later, some not arriving until January, by which time they are thoroughly intermingled with the winter steelhead runs. Although considerable time may pass between the appearance of the first and last fish in the spawning run, the great majority of fish arrive all at once in a large burst, usually within the space of a week or two. Their schools may be seen restlessly prowling the beaches, waiting for the right tide, and when it comes they rush to the river's mouth, splashing, rolling, and leaping as they go, and head upstream as quickly as they can.

Some chum salmon stocks remain bright longer than others, but most have begun changing into their spawning colors by the time they first come within reach of estuary anglers. Their bodies usually have a bronze or olive cast, with large splotches of crimson or gray along the flanks, giving them a mottled appearance that has prompted the nickname "calico salmon" in some quarters. Male fish often display a pronounced kype on their lower jaw, and both male and female adults are typically short and stout in conformation. Visually they are not nearly as appealing as a well-conditioned coho, which is certainly one reason they are less popular among anglers. Their meat also is not considered the equal of coho, chinook, or sockeye salmon, and according to tradition chum were called "dog salmon" because Indians fed them to their dogs.

The chum's primary appeal to anglers is its scrappy nature; it does not fight with the same wild abandon as the coho, but it does fight with amazing strength and endurance. The chum is a real slugger, with no quarter asked and none given, and an angler who hooks one on a fly rod definitely has his or her hands full.

The great swarms of hatchery-produced chum that try to squeeze into the little streams entering Hood Canal also draw swarms of fishermen, and it is not unusual to see dozens of anglers lined up in "picket fences," especially near the mouth of Finch Creek at Hoodsport, where a large state salmon hatchery is located. Despite the crowding, it is easy

A double "picket fence" of anglers fishing for chum salmon off the mouth of Finch Creek, Hoodsport, Washington. If you think this looks crowded, you should see it on weekends.

to catch fish in these places, and almost everyone does, but such fishing has little esthetic appeal. I would much rather seek chum salmon near the mouth of a river with a native run, one that has never been "enhanced" by hatchery production, which usually means it also has escaped the attention of many anglers. It is true that prospects for success in such places are not as certain; only the odd chum can ever be provoked into striking, so many fish must be present for an angler to have a reasonable chance of hooking one, and the natural runs always seem smaller than those swollen by hatchery production. Nevertheless, for many anglers the chance to fish in natural, uncrowded circumstances more than offsets the lesser chances for success.

Either way, estuary fishing for chum salmon is a rapidly growing sport, one that promises to become ever more important in the future. The chum is more widely distributed than any of the other North American species of Pacific salmon, with populations extending from Northern California to Alaska and as far eastward as Canada's MacKenzie River drainage. And while they have suffered from many of the same "four-H" problems affecting coho salmon, chum stocks in most areas are generally in better shape than coho. This may be partly a result of the chum's preference for spawning in large river systems that are not as vulnerable to damage as the smaller streams used by coho, and partly because they are not so avidly sought by commercial fishermen. Whatever the reasons, their relative abundance is good news for estuary fly fishers.

Pink (Humpback) Salmon

Most numerous of all the Pacific salmon, the pink, *Oncorhynchus gorbuscha*, is also commonly known as the humpback, or "humpie," because of the pronounced hump that forms on the backs of spawning males. As with the chum, its value as an estuarine sport fish has been discovered only recently, especially in Southeast Alaska and British Columbia. As also with the chum, this developing fishery is at least partly a result of the success of enhancement programs, although numerous wild runs are fished.

Pinks spawn in the lowest reaches of coastal streams, sometimes even in tidewater. They have a two-year life cycle, and in the southern part of their range, including Puget Sound and Hood Canal, the great majority of runs

It's not often you see water as calm as this. A foggy morning on the Sechelt Peninsula.

occur only in odd-numbered years. Farther north, in British Columbia and Alaskan waters, the strongest runs historically have been in even-numbered years, followed by smaller runs in odd-numbered years, but enhancement efforts have succeeded in creating annual runs of almost equal size in some areas. This increased availability accounts in part for the pink's recent popularity among sport fishermen in British Columbia and Alaska.

Spawning usually occurs in September and October and the eggs may hatch as early as December or as late as early March, depending on water temperatures. Fry emerge from the gravel in April or May and start moving into salt water almost immediately. Their migrating schools are popular targets for feeding Dolly Varden char in the lower rivers or sea-run cutthroat in the estuaries. The young salmon themselves begin feeding as soon as they reach the estuaries, but they do not linger; instead, they head directly out to sea and begin their feeding migration, which takes them into the Gulf of Alaska. They feed mainly on euphasid shrimp and other crustaceans.

After a full year of ocean feeding, a mature pink salmon may weigh anywhere from three to seven pounds. A well-conditioned adult, just beginning its homeward migration, is a very attractive fish, quite similar in appearance to the coho; typically it will be deep blue along its back with silvery sides and a clean white belly. But a pink salmon is easily distinguished from a coho by its very small scales and the presence of large black elliptical spots on its back and tail fin.

The homeward migration begins in late spring and proceeds southward along the coast, where returning schools are prime targets for commercial fishermen. Like chum, they are considered inferior in quality to coho, chinook, or sockeye salmon, but their great numbers at least partly compensate for their lesser commercial worth.

In Southeast Alaska, mature pinks begin moving into the estuaries in late June and by early July they can be caught by beach-wading anglers. Their arrival in British Columbia waters is a little later, but they begin entering the shallow inner waters of the estuaries as early as July. August, however, is the prime time for fly fishers; during that month dense schools of pinks come within easy casting range from the beach. Leaping or porpoising fish often reveal the presence of these schools.

Pinks begin showing in Washington waters in August of odd-numbered years and reach peak abundance in September. The largest runs are to North Puget Sound rivers, such as the Skagit and Stillaguamish, and fish bound for these streams come within easy reach of anglers fishing off the western beaches of Whidbey Island or on the mainland from Mukilteo northward.

A well-conditioned pink hooked on a light fly rod is likely to make a surprisingly strong initial run, taking many yards of backing from the reel, and it is perhaps this characteristic response that makes them most appealing as gamefish. They also fight with unusual tenacity for their size, and while they are among the smallest Pacific salmon, their stubborn nature makes them an adversary worthy of respect.

In the semifinal stage of their migration, as they pass through the estuaries, most pinks remain bright and attractive, although some males may begin swelling with the first signs of their characteristic humpbacked shape. But their brightness fades quickly as they prepare to enter their native streams, which they do as early as August in the north or as late as October in the south. By the time they press into fresh water, or very soon thereafter, their once-handsome silver-blue coloration gives way to dirty brown or gray. The males quickly develop their exaggerated humpbacked shapes; simultaneously, their lower jaws become grotesquely hooked, and by the time they are ready for spawning they are thoroughly disagreeable-looking fish, ugly caricatures of their former selves. Even in this shape, they may still be caught on flies in rivers, but they are hardly attractive targets, and often look as if they may fall apart before an angler can get them to the beach. The time to take them is when they are still clean and bright and at their best, in the estuaries.

The natural range of the pink salmon extends all the way to Northern California, but populations tend to be of only token size south of Puget Sound, not large enough to support significant fisheries. From Puget Sound northward, however, estuary fly fishing for pink salmon continues growing rapidly in popularity and importance, despite the lack of significant even-year runs south of British Columbia.

You see all sorts of strange things in the estuaries.

Chinook (King) Salmon

Largest of all the Pacific salmon, the chinook, *Oncorhynchus tshawytscha*, is known by several other names, including tyee (usually applied to fish weighing more than 30 pounds), spring (a spring-run fish), king, or blackmouth (usually an immature fish). It reaches a maximum weight of more than a hundred pounds, although most adult chinook are of much smaller size.

Throughout its great range, which extends all the way from the Sacramento River in California to tributaries of the Arctic Ocean in Northern Alaska, the chinook employs a variety of different life-history strategies. It prefers major river systems, and some stocks migrate far inland to spawn; because of this, their offspring, which emerge in the spring, must necessarily spend considerable time—even as much as a year—working their way downstream to salt water, feeding and growing as they go. Other stocks spawn close to salt water; their offspring leave the river with little delay and spend several months feeding in the estuaries. Salt marshes and eelgrass beds are especially important habitats for these young migrants, called "ocean-type" chinook, and with the abundant estuarine food stocks at their disposal they usually grow much more rapidly than their riverine counterparts. Even so, they generally do not attain sufficient size to enter the sport catch before they begin their high-seas migration.

Migratory behavior and timing varies among different stocks, but generally the migration is northward, then westward into the far reaches of the Bering Sea. As with coho, however, a small percentage of each year class of chinook salmon appears to residualize in sheltered waters like Puget Sound, and some of these resident populations have been significantly enhanced by holding chinook juveniles in hatcheries past their normal smolting stage. These resident fish provide an important sport fishery for "blackmouth," but they do not attain sizes similar to those of ocean-going chinook.

The latter may spend several years feeding at sea before instinct summons them home. As with most other elements in the life cycle of the chinook, there is considerable variation in the timing of these homeward migrations. Some fish return to their native rivers in the early spring, others during summer, and many in the fall. Southern rivers are more likely to have multiple runs than northern rivers, where the long winters limit favorable conditions for spawning, hatching,

and rearing. No matter when they occur, virtually all these runs historically have been fished heavily by both sport and commercial fishermen. Many years of intensive harvest, coupled with severe habitat degradation—mostly caused by dams on major river systems, such as the Columbia—have brought numerous runs of wild chinook to the point of extinction, or in some cases beyond it. The huge, 50-pound-plus salmon that once returned to rivers flowing into Puget Sound, for example, are now only fading memories in the minds of old-timers.

But anglers still avidly seek chinook salmon wherever they are found. A well-conditioned returning chinook adult is a very handsome, powerfully built fish, typically blocky in shape, thick and deep with chrome-colored flanks and a deep blue-green back covered by a fine spray of black spots. Upon entering fresh water, some stocks retain their brightness longer than others—a trait that seems especially common among spring- and summer-run fish—and it is not unusual for sea-bright chinook to be caught by anglers fishing well upstream from salt water. But inevitably their colors do begin to fade, with male fish becoming a dirty red and females a sort of bronze color as they approach spawning. Depending upon run timing and location, actual spawning may take place anywhere from late August to early December.

Chinook salmon are deeper-ranging fish than any of the other species of Pacific salmon, and that fact, coupled with the scattered timing of their spawning runs, limits their accessibility to estuary fly fishers. With the proper tackle and tactics, it is sometimes possible to take resident chinook on flies in the deeper portions of sheltered bays and inlets, and these provide the bulk of the catch among estuary anglers. However, it is also often possible to catch chinook in the estuaries during the big fall runs. Small "jack" chinook—precocious male fish of 1 1/2 to 5 pounds—are the easiest to catch, but persistent anglers have an opportunity to take much larger adults as they pass through the shallow estuaries.

A returning chinook of any size provides excellent sport on a light fly rod, and a large one may offer the angling experience of a lifetime. These great fish are sought seasonally by thousands of anglers from Northern California to Alaska, providing the most widespread recreational fishery of any species of Pacific salmon.

IV
TROUT AND CHAR IN
NORTHWEST ESTUARIES

In addition to the salmon, Northwest estuaries are home to migrating sea-run cutthroat trout, steelhead, and Dolly Varden char in their seasons. These fish always have been fewer in numbers than the salmon and their movements have always been more subtle and secretive, so in most cases they have never been sought by anglers with quite the same fervor as the salmon.

The cutthroat and Dolly Varden are relative homebodies, the least anadromous of all the Pacific salmonids. They may spend more time in fresh water then they do in salt, and when they do journey to salt water they never stray very far from the mouths of their home rivers—a habit that makes them of special interest to estuary fly fishers. They also have the least commercial value of all the salmonids—literally none—so they have largely escaped the notice of researchers; less is known about them than any of their cousins. Yet the cutthroat, in at least some parts of its range, provides a popular estuary sport fishery throughout the year.

The steelhead traditionally has been a very important sport fish in rivers, but little research has been done concerning its behavior and movements in the estuaries and few anglers are aware of its value as an estuary fish. That's hardly surprising, considering that few anglers fish the estuaries during winter months when the largest steelhead runs occur; some who do, however, have discovered that at certain times, under certain conditions, estuaries can offer extraordinary angling for these splendid fish.

For most of this century, the sea-run or coastal cutthroat and the steelhead trout were classified in the genus *Salmo*, but research findings presented in 1988 indicated both fish are more closely related to the Pacific salmon, *Oncorhynchus*, than previously thought, so they were reclassified as part of the genus *Oncorhynchus* and both now go by that awkward taxonomic name. In the lexicon of anglers, however, it seems likely they will always be considered trout, and they are so identified here.

Sea-Run Cutthroat

Of all the Pacific salmonids, the sea-run or coastal cutthroat, *Oncorhynchus clarki clarki*, is the least abundant and the longest-lived. It also has the most complex life history and is the species most dependent on estuaries. Secretive in its ways, it is never as spectacularly visible as any of the Pacific salmon, nor can it compare with them either in size or performance at the end of an angler's line. Yet it is a fish that seems to have a way of working its way into an angler's heart, just as it works its way silently along the beaches of the estuaries that are its chosen habitat, and it has become the favorite fish of many Northwest estuary fly fishers.

One reason it enjoys this status is because the cutthroat is more than just a seasonal fish in some areas of its broad natural range; in those areas—Puget Sound, Hood Canal, and some of the sheltered waters of southern British Columbia—it remains in the estuaries throughout all or most of the year, at least in some numbers, and in these locations it has become the closest thing to a year-round fish for estuary anglers.

Another reason anglers hold the sea-run cutthroat in such high regard is its ready willingness to take a fly. Although it can be coy on occasion, most of the time it will attack a fly—virtually any fly—with an honest exuberance and enthusiasm that seems lacking in other fish. It matters little if the fly is bright or dark, wet or dry—an eager cutthroat will take it anyway.

Once hooked, a sea-run seldom displays any of the fireworks commonly associated with salmon or steelhead, but it always fights stubbornly, usually in a series of short, strong rushes. Sometimes sea-runs may thrash about noisily on the surface, throwing spray, and occasionally they jump to incredible heights, although this is uncommon.

Adult sea-runs are not large, rarely exceeding four pounds in weight, but their aggressiveness, stubborn fight, and attractive appearance—a pleasing blend of olive and silver, fine black spots and yellowish fins—make them an

This well-conditioned sea-run cutthroat fell to a shrimp imitation on a winter day in Puget Sound. It was released after posing.

ideal fish for light fly rods. They are also wonderful table fish, perhaps the best tasting of all seagoing salmonids, but in most parts of their range they are among the last remaining wild trout, far too valuable to be killed for the table or any other purpose.

Of the 14 recognized subspecies of cutthroat trout, the coastal cutthroat is by far the most widely distributed. Its range extends from California's Eel River to Prince William Sound, Alaska (although, oddly, cutthroat are missing from some areas of the Queen Charlotte Islands off the British Columbia Coast). As researchers have noted, this distribution coincides quite closely with that of the native coastal rain forests, suggesting an ecological relationship. Many different stocks have evolved over this broad range, and they employ a wide variety of life-history strategies. The coastal cutthroat seems to have great talent for adapting to the circumstances in which it finds itself, from near-glacial environments in Alaska to small streams draining directly into the Pacific Ocean in Northern California.

Sea-run cutthroat spawn in the smallest tributaries, little short-run streams that drain directly to saltwater bays, or capillary-sized creeks that flow almost unnoticed into larger streams or full-fledged rivers. Typically these are slow-moving, low-gradient streams or sloughs, often flowing through marshes or meadows. Adult cutthroat push all the way to their headwaters, frequently spawning farther upstream than the coho salmon or other salmonids with which they share many of these tributaries.

There are countless numbers of these little coastal creeks and tributaries, and the cutthroat populations that inhabit them display considerable differences in the timing of their spawning runs. Researchers have observed that wild fish captured in salt water and held in pens ripened at different times so it was difficult to find males and females simultaneously ready for spawning. Since these fish were captured randomly, it seems probable they represented several different stocks, underscoring the notion that different stocks spawn at different times. Studies of sea-run cutthroat in Puget Sound, Hood Canal, and southern British Columbia tend to confirm this, having identified separate fall and winter spawning runs. It appears some stocks may spawn as early as November, others in January or February, still others in the spring.

The late Alan Pratt, doing what he loved to do. The scene is a small estuary near the north end of Hood Canal.

When they do spawn, sea-run cutthroat usually dig their redds in patches of small gravel in six to eighteen inches of water; often they select the tail-cuts of pools for this purpose. There is a minimum of pre-spawning ritual, and the spawning act itself is the same as that for any trout: The female, having dug the redd to her satisfaction, spills her cargo of red-orange eggs into the gravel while the straining male simultaneously covers them with milt. A healthy, well-conditioned female may carry slightly less than a thousand eggs per pound of weight, although the eggs of older, heavier, repeat-spawning females tend to be larger and more numerous, and have a better chance of survival.

When the spawning act is complete, the female moves upstream to dig another nest, dislodging gravel that settles over the fertilized eggs she has just left. Oxygen-rich water flows freely through the small, loosely packed stones and circulates around the eggs, keeping them alive.

As with other salmonids, the gestation period of sea-run cutthroat eggs depends on water temperature, determined not only by the geographic location of the stream but also when the eggs were deposited. Eggs laid in the spring are likely to develop more rapidly in the warmer temperatures of that season, even in northern climes, than eggs deposited in the frigid short days of winter. Overall, the gestation period probably averages about six or seven weeks before the eggs hatch into tiny alevins. These remain buried in the gravel another week or two until their yolks are absorbed; then hunger drives them out into the open stream as free-swimming fry. Their emergence may occur as early as March in warmer southern waters, as late as May in northern streams.

The fry usually average about an inch long when they emerge, not yet large or strong enough to keep station in the current, so they seek slower flows along the margins of the stream. There they remain for several weeks, feeding and gaining strength until they are finally able to move out into the current and establish territories. In streams where coho salmon also spawn, cutthroat fry usually find that young coho already have occupied the best feeding and resting stations. The coho, having emerged earlier, also enjoy an advantage in size; they force the smaller cutthroat into riffles and runs where they have more difficulty finding food and must expend more energy to obtain it. Juvenile steelhead similarly displace young cutthroat from the most favorable feeding and resting areas, and this ruthless competition among species is a major factor contributing to cutthroat fry mortality.

In streams where cutthroat are the sole occupants, they are free to choose the most advantageous feeding and resting places. They seek the margins of pools and feed on the nymphs and larvae of tiny insects, or on small aquatic or terrestrial adults. But only rarely is there enough such food to go around; most cutthroat spawning streams are cold and acidic, with relatively small insect populations. As a result, competition for food among cutthroat fry is fierce and mortality is high. Relentless predation by mergansers, herons, kingfishers, or larger fish also takes a grim toll of young fish, and others die when they become stranded in drying potholes during the heat of summer. By September, of all the fry that emerged from the gravel in the spring, only a few survivors will remain. Most of these will measure less than an inch and a half long, but they will be starting to show the first bright scales along their flanks.

At some point during the fall or winter months these little fish will be joined by adult cutthroat returning from the estuaries to spawn, and although feeding is not the first priority of the returning fish, they add yet another element to the competition for food—and this, coming in the harsh, lean months of winter, inevitably exacts another toll of fry. Yet there are still survivors, and by the following spring they have grown into strong and sturdy little fish, tempered by all the stern tests that nature can devise. After a full year of life they average about two and a half inches long, with flanks plainly marked by a series of dark bars known as parr marks.

Now they settle into a seasonal routine that will govern their lives for at least another year, and for many even longer. As seasons change, as each new crop of fry emerges from the gravel, as the stream rises and falls in rhythm with wet or dry weather, these yearling fish move upstream or down, seeking the most favorable resting and feeding stations and the most comfortable temperatures and flows.

By the end of its second year of stream residence, a healthy juvenile cutthroat may be five and a half inches long. Its movements sometimes take it as far downstream as tidewater, as if in rehearsal for the migration it will later make. It may remain there for some time, but eventually returns upstream. There it congregates with others of its kind in slow, deep pools with irregular shores and undercut banks, or in pockets formed by root balls or snags that offer protection against strong winter flows.

The smolting instinct, which finally triggers a young cutthroat's urge to leave its native stream and enter salt water, seizes different fish at different times. Laboratory experiments have shown that even very young cutthroat are able to make the transition from fresh to salt water without difficulty, so the timing of the smolt stage apparently is not related to any physical change or maturation required for the purpose. Instead, it appears to have more to do with the size of the fish, as if evolution had programmed it to reach a certain size before leaving its native stream and venturing into the estuaries. Still, there is great diversity in both the size and age at which these fish begin their seaward passage. A few may do so after only a single year of in-stream life, many more after two years, and the greatest number after three. Yet some wait four years before making their first migration, a few even five, and there are some recorded instances of six-year-old cutthroat making their initial foray to the sea.

This great variety in smolting behavior makes generalizations difficult, but a couple of patterns are discernible. One is that smolting tends to be earlier—usually at age two—in streams that flow into sheltered waters, and later—usually at age three or four—in streams that flow to the open sea. This stands to reason, for older, larger smolts probably have a better chance of survival in the rough-and-tumble world of the ocean surf. Another pattern is that cutthroat tend to smolt at an earlier age in the southern part of their range than in the north. Undoubtedly this is because they grow more rapidly in the warmer streams of California, Oregon, and Washington—and thus reach smolting size earlier—than they do in British Columbia or Alaska. Steelhead also share this trait.

Yet there the patterns end. No matter when smolting occurs, there are nearly always some individuals that do not smolt at all. These may take up permanent residence upstream, or migrate up and downstream but never into salt water. Some streams also have natural barriers, such as waterfalls, that prevent headwater populations from mingling with downstream stocks—yet these isolated headwater populations sometimes contribute sea-run fish through so-called "one-way migrations" in which individual fish find their way downstream to salt water, but are prevented by the natural barrier from returning to spawn with the population that originally gave them life. This great variety of behavior among local coastal cutthroat stocks may be a sort of survival mechanism, assuring that even if catastrophe strikes there will always be at least some fish alive somewhere in the system—the headwaters, the mainstem, or the estuaries—to perpetuate the species.

For those fish that do migrate to sea, the smolting instinct always asserts itself in the spring, and the first cutthroat begin dropping downstream toward the estuary as early as March. Their numbers grow steadily, peaking in mid-May throughout the cutthroat's southern range and in mid-June for Alaskan waters. After the initial surge, there are always stragglers that continue working their way downstream as late as July.

Usually the larger smolts are first to leave the stream. Like their smaller counterparts that come later, they form schools and move downstream at night. Their progress may be halted by a sudden rise in streamflow from heavy rain or melting snow, or a sudden drop caused by a late spell of cold weather; either will cause them to halt and remain where they are until the flow stabilizes. Then they will resume their journey, and in such fits and starts they make their way downstream until they feel the first lift of a rising tide.

Rarely are there very many of them. Where it has been possible for researchers to make accurate counts of smolt escapement from spawning tributaries, they have found the numbers almost invariably small, usually less than a thousand smolts from any single tributary. Large river systems may collectively produce several thousand smolts, but only a small number will come from each tributary.

After the long confinement of their native stream, the smolts' entry into the estuary can only seem like a passage into another world. The young fish cluster in schools, varying in size from two or three fish to many dozens, and set out to explore their new environment. Their arrival in salt water takes place on the eve of the most productive season of the year, a time when estuarine plants and animals are multiplying and growing rapidly, and the young cutthroat quickly begin feeding on the wealth of food they find along the beaches and in the coastal bays—isopods, amphipods, shrimp, crab larvae, perhaps even salmon fry, sand lance, or other small forage fish.

Sea-run cutthroat lack the bold wanderlust of steelhead or salmon, and most never travel very far from the mouth of their home rivers—yet here again there are marked differences in behavior. Radiotelemetry experiments in Southeast Alaska tracked sea-run cutthroat as far as 25 or 30 miles in salt water, but they always hugged the shoreline closely, keeping within the intertidal zone, and never crossed large, open, deep bodies of water. Off the Oregon coast, on the other hand, sea-run cutthroat have been captured in nets as far as 40 miles out to sea. These drastic differences in behavior are almost certainly due to equally drastic differences in environment. In Southeast Alaska—as well as in Washington and British Columbia—the convolut-

Volunteers clear gravel in a stream before planting sea-run cutthroat eggs in plastic Vibert boxes.

ed coastline, with its hundreds of small estuaries, protected channels and bays, and countless miles of gentle, sloping gravel beach, provides ideal sheltered feeding habitat for cutthroat, and in most cases they have no need to cross large, open bodies of water. But the Oregon and Northern California coasts have mostly smaller estuaries that offer minimal food and shelter, and their ocean beaches are continually swept by wild, pounding surf, an inhospitable environment for cutthroat. In these areas cutthroat avoid the intertidal zone; instead they follow currents in the ocean, usually six to twelve miles from shore, although some range much farther out to sea. Each case is an example of cutthroat adapting as necessary for survival, proving again they are the ultimate pragmatists among fish.

Soon after reaching salt water, young cutthroat shed their parr marks and the colorful livery of their streamside years and assume the bright armor of sea-run fish. Their sides gleam with fine scales, each a miniature mirror reflecting silvery glints, and these yield in turn to dark forest green along the fish's back. Both back and sides are covered with a fine spray of irregularly shaped black spots, and when light strikes their flanks at a certain angle a faint flush of olive may be seen. Some fish display isolated bright yellow spots, and their pectoral and ventral fins are often yellow too. Beneath its jaw each cutthroat wears the twin marks that are the badges of the species, but these are usually faint in sea-run fish, like a pair of old, well-healed scars. Their overall color scheme is well adapted to the estuaries, with their own tints of green and olive, black and yellow.

The young cutthroat grow rapidly, typically gaining an inch every summer month they spend in salt water. But even as they seek their own food, they remain food for others, including a host of new predators—harbor seals, sea lions, salmon, cormorants, murres, fish-eating ducks, dogfish, hake, and adult salmon. So their existence remains as perilous as ever.

The sea-run's search for food often takes it to the uppermost margins of the tide, within a few feet of shore, sometimes in water so shallow it scarcely covers them. As they grow larger, sea-run cutthroat become more aggressively piscivorous, turning to other fish as the mainstay of their diet. In the sheltered waters of Washington, British Columbia, and Alaska, favorite targets include the Pacific sand lance during summer, migrating three-spine stickleback in the fall, and candlefish (eulachon) in the winter. Pillbugs, scuds, and small true shrimp also remain important, especially during fall and winter months. Ocean-dwelling cutthroat along the California, Oregon, and outer Washington coasts rely heavily on the northern anchovy, but also take herring, greenling, and other juvenile salmonids, along with copepods and mollusks. Their diets overlap considerably with those of coho and chinook salmon, so the competition among species that began in fresh water continues in the salt.

A Vibert box (not visible) full of sea-run cutthroat eggs is placed in the gravel of a stream flowing into Hood Canal. This method of trying to augment sea-run populations has since been abandoned.

At the end of their first full summer of saltwater feeding, most cutthroat return to their rivers of origin. Some do this even though they are not yet sexually mature and ready to spawn, and it has been suggested they are biologically programmed to take advantage of the feeding opportunities presented by the fall salmon-spawning runs, when loose salmon eggs may be abundant. Others enter fresh water on the first leg of a journey in search of winter refuge. Whatever the motivation, the movement begins as early as late July and continues until early fall, usually peaking in late August or early September. The timing apparently is related to the distance adult cutthroat must travel to their spawning grounds; those that spawn in the tributaries of large river systems usually have farther to go than those spawning in short-run coastal streams, so they begin their journey earlier. It is this migration, which traditionally occurs in many rivers about the time of the first harvest, that has given sea-run cutthroat the local name of "harvest trout" in parts of its range.

Yet not all cutthroat return to fresh water in the fall—or, if they do, not all remain there very long. There is more confusion over this aspect of their behavior than any other part of their life history. Some of this confusion probably is a residual effect of one of the first studies of sea-run cutthroat behavior.

That study, by the biologist R.D. Giger, concluded that Oregon coastal cutthroat always winter in fresh water, never in the salt. This conclusion, undoubtedly correct for Oregon coastal cutthroat, seems to have stuck in the minds of succeeding generations of biologists, leading to a general assumption that what is true for sea-run cutthroat in Oregon must be true for sea-run cutthroat everywhere. Given all the other observed variations in sea-run cutthroat behavior, this would seem to be a very questionable assumption, but it has been enough to deter most biologists from looking for other patterns of winter behavior. It also has kept them from acknowledging what anglers in South Puget Sound, Hood Canal, and Southern British Columbia have known for many years: Sea-run cutthroat in those waters do *not* spend the winter in fresh water; many remain in the estuaries. In fact, winter is the preferred time for many anglers to fish for sea-runs in those waters.

Just what is going on here? The answer, once again, is that sea-run cutthroat have adapted to local differences in their environment. Oregon coastal cutthroat apparently return to fresh water not only to spawn but also to seek refuge from the unfriendly winter environment of the ocean and its fierce storms; many of them winter in beaver ponds where these are available and accessible.

Sea-runs in Southeast Alaska also seek winter refuge in fresh water, but they do so with a slightly different twist. These fish ascend streams with lakes in their headwaters and spend the winter in those lakes; then, in the spring, they return briefly to salt water before seeking their home streams to spawn. Whether this behavior is characteristic of all Southeast Alaska sea-runs, or whether some winter in streams or remain in the estuaries during all or part of the winter, is not known.

Sea-run cutthroat in Northern Puget Sound exhibit yet another pattern of behavior. They seek out large rivers such as the Skagit, Snohomish, and Stillaguamish, enter them in the late summer or early fall and apparently remain over winter—or at least many do. But in South Puget Sound, Hood Canal, the waters around British Columbia's Sechelt Peninsula, and perhaps in other locations, cutthroat remain abundant in salt water through the winter. Either many of them do not enter fresh water at all, or they return very quickly to salt water after having done so.

Why should things be different in these waters? One reason is that the waters themselves are different. All are protected estuaries, sheltered from the full fury of winter storms and surf. With few exceptions, they are fed mostly by small, short-run streams rather than major rivers. Finally, all enjoy a temperate climate, which assures a relatively plentiful supply of food even during winter. Taken together, these factors offer a favorable year-round environment for cutthroat, probably one more friendly in winter than any they could find in the fresh waters accessible to them. So they stand to gain no metabolic or survival advantage by wintering in fresh water.

It seems worth noting that many of the fish I have caught during winter months in these waters have been small, less than 12 inches in length, and based on their average size and an examination of the scales of some individuals, I believe most were fish in their first year of saltwater residence—in other words, fish that entered salt water the previous spring and remained after their initial summer of feeding, either without returning to fresh water at all or returning for only a very short time. However, I have also taken many larger bright fish during winter months; some of these undoubtedly were maiden fish, others possibly "skip-spawners"—fish that had spawned a year previously and returned to salt water for a year without ripening to spawn again—although this is merely supposition. Some also were clearly kelts, fish that had spawned recently and returned to the estuary. Usually the kelts begin to show up in late November or early December, with a second, larger group in February, and those times coincide closely with the timing of the early- and late-entry spawning runs researchers have documented in Puget Sound and Hood Canal. Their numbers are never large, however; my records for the past 25 years show kelts accounted for a little more than 10 percent of the fish I have caught in February, much less in other months.

Obviously there is still much to be learned about the movements of sea-run cutthroat in fall or winter, especially those of immature fish coming off their first summer in salt water. Spawning fish, fortunately, are another matter; while the timing of their runs may vary widely, their behavior once the run begins is relatively straightforward.

A sea-run cutthroat that is ready to spawn must return to fresh water for the purpose. Whether it does so in fall, winter, or spring, its appearance changes quickly after it enters a stream. The silvery flanks lose much of their luster and take on a more obvious flush of olive or pale yellow, the fine black spots become larger and more prominent, and the twin cutthroat marks brighten and turn crimson; only the dark-green color of the cutthroat's back remains unchanged. In this freshwater livery the sea-run cutthroat is a truly beautiful fish, at least for a time, but as it nears spawning its features and colors become exaggerated until they cross the line between beauty and ugliness; then the fish becomes dark and gravid.

Cutthroat spawning migrations are usually short in time and often in distance, but adult sea-runs still lose a substantial portion of their body weight in spawning and their mortality rate is high (although not as high as among other salmonids). Studies in Washington and Oregon have shown that approximately 40 percent of spawning cutthroat may survive to spawn a second time, about 17 percent a third time, perhaps 12 percent a fourth time. Occasionally they skip a year between spawning migrations.

After spawning, some fish remain in fresh water and seek winter refuge areas, returning to salt water only after spring has come, while others hurry back down to the estuaries. No matter when they return to salt water, they feed ravenously and usually recover rapidly from their spawning ordeal, again changing colors in a reversal of the process that occurred before spawning; soon they are once again handsome, silvery, sea-run fish.

After its initial spawning migration is complete and it has returned to the estuary, an adult sea-run cutthroat has completed one full cycle of its life. It then settles into a more-or-less regular pattern of summer estuary feeding, usually followed by another spawning migration in the fall or winter, another return to the estuary if it survives, and repeats this cycle for as long as it lives. In some cases, that may be for as long as ten years.

A fish that spends its first two years in fresh water before smolting may grow to a length of 18 inches and a weight of two or three pounds by the time it is six years old, but fish of larger size are definitely the exception; a four-pounder may be an angler's lifetime catch, and a sea-run cutthroat of five pounds or more is rare indeed.

In October, 1995, fisheries scientists and researchers got together in Reedsport, Oregon, to compare notes on sea-run cutthroat for the first time. The three-day seminar produced more questions than answers, clearly revealing the many gaps remaining in our collective knowledge of this fish. As one speaker observed, "One problem with analyzing the data is that we don't have any."

It was equally obvious that biologists had waited far too long to begin talking about these fish, for there were many reports of cutthroat stocks in serious trouble or others already extinct. Several Lower Columbia River stocks, including those of the Wind and Klickitat Rivers and many smaller tributaries below Bonneville Dam, were reported extinct; others, including the native cutthroat of the Hood River, were described at high risk of extinction. Many Oregon and Northern California coastal stocks were reported in similar trouble, including the cutthroat of the Umpqua River, which flows into the ocean at Reedsport—one reason the symposium was held there.

Numerous causes were cited for these declines. Not surprisingly, they included the same "four-Hs" that have damaged other salmonid stocks, although sea-run cutthroat probably have suffered less from hydroelectric dams and certainly less from commercial harvests than salmon and steelhead. But some stocks have been damaged by excessive recreational harvest, others by hatchery programs, and many by "development" or other land-use changes, especially logging. The small, fragile nature of their spawning streams, their extended freshwater residence compared with other salmonids, and their dependence upon in-stream pools all make sea-run populations especially vulnerable to damage from logging or similarly disruptive activities. Yet sea-runs have rarely been considered in environmental or land-use studies because they have little or no commercial value and their population numbers are low relative to other species. If they are considered at all, usually it is after the damage already has been done.

Volunteers clip the fins of hatchery-reared sea-run cutthroat fry. After the fish are released in the wild, the missing fin will identify them as being of hatchery origin.

Such after-the-fact studies have shown conclusively that cutthroat population densities are lower in watersheds that have been logged heavily. Logging impacts either kill cutthroat outright or force them into more intensive competition with other salmonids for food and space, almost always to the cutthroat's disadvantage. In Washington's Grays River basin, for example, timber harvesting between 1938 and 1990 resulted in loss of 69 percent of the critical in-stream pool habitat that existed before 1938. Even higher percentages have been recorded in other river basins.

These kinds of changes also lead to more subtle and insidious problems, including an increase in hybridization of cutthroat with steelhead. This occurs even under natural conditions, since cutthroat and steelhead share overlapping habitats, but rarely to the extent that the genetic identity of either species is in danger of being compromised. But increased rates of hybridization were found in two streams where logging or other disturbances disrupted natural habitats or caused a decrease in the numbers of one parent species, and researchers concluded this could be a contributing factor in the overall decline of native coastal cutthroat populations.

Nor is habitat destruction confined only to the streams where cutthroat spawn and rear. Diking and filling, channelization, dredging, gravel mining, shoreline changes, construction of jetties and marinas, and dredge spoil disposal have reduced or destroyed cutthroat habitat in many estuaries. Major changes in weather patterns during the past 20 years also are suspected of contributing to the decline of sea-run populations throughout their southern range. These changes have caused significant ocean warming and a decline in the upwelling of cold, nutrient-rich water off the coast, plus a sort of persistent, low-level El Nino condition off the Oregon and Washington coasts since 1990. Counts of sea-run cutthroat returning to the Lower Columbia and Umpqua Rivers have shown consistent declines during the period since these changes were first observed.

In the Umpqua River, a record of the number of sea-run cutthroat migrating over Winchester Dam has been kept for many years, giving a longer-term picture of the health of the population than is available in most other watersheds. From 1946 to 1956, these counts ranged from 400 to 1,800 adult fish a year, with an average of about 950. By 1960, however, the number had declined to fewer than 100 fish a year. Hatchery cutthroat were introduced to the system in 1961, and only twice since then has the run exceeded 100 fish. In 1993, only 29 fish returned, and in 1992 and 1994 there were none at all. These drastic declines prompted conservation groups to petition for endangered species classification of the Umpqua cutthroat.

What caused these catastrophic declines? The Umpqua cutthroat have been subjected to all the perils mentioned previously, plus a few that may be unique only to them. Umpqua River cutthroat are known to penetrate farther inland than any other stock, thus increasing their chances of exposure to environmental problems and habitat changes along the way. They also have had to compete with many exotic species. Historically, only seven species of fish, including sea-run cutthroat, are believed to have been native to the Umpqua basin, but 18 other species have since been introduced. These include smallmouth

A netful of anesthetized sea-run cutthroat fry, ready for fin clipping.

and striped bass, both of which are known to feed on juvenile salmonids.

Extremely high and rapidly fluctuating pH levels also have been found in several upstream tributaries of the Umpqua system, exceeding 9.0 in some cases (the state standard is between 6.5, slightly acidic, and 8.5, somewhat alkaline). The highest levels, above 9.0, usually occur in afternoons when the sun is on the water, falling again when the stream is in shadow. Thick algae exposed to sunlight is suspected as the cause of the high pH levels, and both algae and high pH are evidence of degraded habitat from logging, including removal of normal shade cover and increased nutrient run-off.

In one of these tributaries, Jackson Creek, high and rapidly fluctuating pH levels were identified as a cause of stress leading to low egg-to-smolt survival of spring chinook salmon. It seems probable cutthroat populations have suffered similarly where affected by the same conditions.

The geographic location of the Umpqua basin, in the heart of the area most affected by recent changes in climate and ocean conditions, also may place its cutthroat at greater risk of extinction than populations in northern watersheds where these conditions do not apply.

So the outlook for Umpqua River cutthroat appears gloomy. But not all the news at the Reedsport symposium was bad; many sea-run cutthroat populations, especially in the northern part of their range, are believed in healthy condition—although little is known about most of them. An area-by-area rundown, from south to north:

California

Cutthroat populations have been identified in 186 named streams, seven unnamed streams, and at least four coastal lagoons in Northern California. Most of the streams are small, and many are tributaries of larger systems; 40 percent are in the Smith River drainage. The average penetration of sea-run populations is 20 miles inland, but in streams near the Oregon border they extend inland as far as 75 miles. The entire population of sea-runs in California is estimated at less than the historic population of the Alsea River drainage in Oregon, and they have never had a large following among California anglers.

The Eel River drainage appears the southern limit of the species' distribution. Sedimentation has filled in much of the Eel River estuary and slough habitat, and sea-runs are now rare in the delta, but fair populations of what apparently are mostly resident cutthroat still exist in the forested portions of small tributaries as far as 10 miles inland.

Cutthroat are rarely encountered in the open waters of Humboldt Bay, but are found in the bay's estuaries and tributaries. However, many of these tributaries have been damaged by habitat changes, although not as badly as those of the Eel.

The Mad River supports cutthroat up to 10 miles inland and populations are found in nine tributaries, but sea-runs are not common in the estuary.

Cutthroat populations have been identified in 23 small streams flowing directly into the ocean, with a total of about 72 miles of habitat. However, many of these streams have migration barriers, and population densities below the barriers are not high. The most important of these streams is the Little River which has a mile-long estuary.

Redwood Creek once was a fine coastal cutthroat stream; cutthroat were found in 23 of its tributaries with 65 miles of habitat. But after the severe 1964 flood, the lower reaches of Redwood Creek were disrupted by construction of flood-control channels; this also removed much of the coastal lagoon. The cutthroat population crashed after these changes, and Redwood Creek now has only about one cutthroat per mile, although population densities in its tributaries are somewhat higher. Recent surveys, based on small samples, show a downward trend in lower river populations and an increase in upstream populations. Part of the Redwood Creek system is now in Redwood National Park, and a road-abrogation program is under way.

The Klamath River estuary is one of the largest along the Northern California coast, and the Klamath River has cutthroat populations in 25 tributaries ranging inland as far as Martin's Ferry. Many downstream tributaries were logged heavily, suffered further damage in the 1964 flood, and still have still not recovered, but recent sampling shows a slight increase in juvenile cutthroat numbers. Anglers take as many as 360 cutthroat a year from the Klamath system.

The Smith River estuary is similar in size—about five miles long—to the Klamath. With its many tributaries, the Smith once had a good sea-run cutthroat population, but it was depleted by angling pressure and damage from the 1964 flood, exacerbated by logging impacts. These impacts were especially bad on the South Fork of the Smith, while the Middle Fork suffered more from highway construction. Both forks are recovering slowly and cutthroat population densities now range from 10 to 22 fish per mile, with a slight upward trend since 1982. Some of these fish are probably sea-runs while others appear to be resident.

Surveys taken on the Smith River during the early 1980s showed anglers were taking as many as 2,000 cutthroat trout a year. The river's total summer population of cutthroat is now estimated at 1,000 fish exceeding 10 inches in length, not including sea-runs that enter the river in late summer or early fall. More recent angling surveys suggest the catch rate remains fairly high, so the bag limit was reduced from five to two fish a day in 1995.

Traditionally, much of California's angling effort for sea-run cutthroat has been directed at populations in coastal lagoons, but these have not fared well in recent years. Clam Beach Lagoon was destroyed by highway development, along with its cutthroat population. Freshwater Lagoon was chemically treated and few cutthroat remain, if any. Big Lagoon is filling with silt from logging in its watershed and suffers from oxygen deficiency in the summer, although it still has a good cutthroat population, especially off Maple Creek.

In 1987, wild cutthroat were collected from Humboldt Bay tributaries for use as breeding stock and their offspring, marked by freeze brands, were planted in Stone Lagoon. These grew to an average length of 14.6 inches after two years. A 1993 sampling program trapped 2,231 fish in the brackish lagoon, of which 84 percent were cutthroat of hatchery origin (the rest were wild cutthroat or steelhead). But stocking ended in May 1993, and the following month vandals breached the sand bar separating the lagoon from the ocean and nearly all the fish escaped. During the 1993-94 season, only 36 adult cutthroat were trapped; in July 1995, sampling attempts took no fish at all.

Oregon

Cutthroat were historically present in virtually all Oregon coastal streams and Lower Columbia River tributaries without migration barriers in their lower reaches. Some river systems, such as the Alsea and Siuslaw, had very large numbers. Angling for these fish became popular as early as the mid-1930s and generated even more effort than fishing for salmon or steelhead. Sea-run cutthroat were of particular interest to fly fishers, who sought them during their annual migrations through the estuaries and into the lower rivers.

Even then people were concerned about the health of sea-run stocks, and state and federal agencies reacted to those concerns by doing things that were thought to be good ideas at the time but which, in retrospect, can only have done more harm than good. The Depression-era Works Progress Administration built a hatchery on the Alsea to augment its wild cutthroat population with hatchery stocks—the first of many such efforts. The state, meanwhile, brought in Yellowstone cutthroat and released them in Willamette Valley streams.

Clipping the pectoral fin of a hatchery-reared sea-run cutthroat. This method of marking fish is sometimes still used where cutthroat hatchery programs remain in operation.

Things have been pretty much downhill ever since, although for many years the decline was gradual; only in the past couple of decades has it become precipitous. The plight of the Umpqua cutthroat, for example, has already been discussed in detail; suffice it to say, with endangered-species classification pending, no angling is permitted for what few fish remain in that system. And the Umpqua is not the only river with such problems.

The Siuslaw River once had one of the largest cutthroat populations of any river system; in 1970, it was estimated at 31,000 fish. By 1994, that number had declined to 340. This catastrophic decline has been accompanied by a parallel decline in angling effort, despite increasing plants of hatchery fish in an effort to sustain the fishery (Giger's pioneering study of sea-run cutthroat reported the hatchery fish were three times more "catchable" than wild fish). From 1967 to 1970, there was an average 31 percent return to the creel from hatchery plants; now the average is only 1.2 percent. The Siuslaw cutthroat may not be as close to extinction as those of the Umpqua system, but they are obviously not far behind.

The pattern in the Alsea River system is unfortunately similar, both in terms of cutthroat populations and angling effort. In the mid-1960s, the Alsea's wild cutthroat population was estimated at 2,600; now it is estimated at 160. In 1969-70, there were an estimated 22 fish per river mile; by 1991-1993 that had declined to 2.2 fish per mile. Studies also indicate more fish are now smolting at age one or two than was the case 30 years ago, and fewer fish now survive to spawn more than once; in 1962, 33 percent of the spawning fish survived to spawn a second time, but by 1990 that rate had declined to 7 percent. These observations suggest significant changes in the age structure of the cutthroat population, which could be due to angler harvest, habitat degradation, or both.

Declines also have been documented in the Wilson River. Giger reported an average of 10.5 cutthroat per pool in the late 1960s; contemporary surveys show 1.2 fish per pool.

The Hood River, a major tributary of the Columbia, holds the easternmost population of anadromous cutthroat in Oregon. As noted previously, these fish are now believed at high risk of extinction. The severe decline or extinction of sea-run stocks in other Lower Columbia tributaries also has been noted. Angler surveys during the 1970s routinely showed annual catches of around 5,000 cutthroat from these waters; by the late 1980s, the number had declined to as little as 500 a year. It is probably even lower now.

Certainly the expansion and growing velocity of timber harvest has had much to do with the disappearance of Oregon's cutthroat. Stocking of hatchery fish also has been

Winter morning on an estuary along British Columbia's Sechelt Peninsula. The peninsula has many estuaries frequented by sea-run cutthroat.

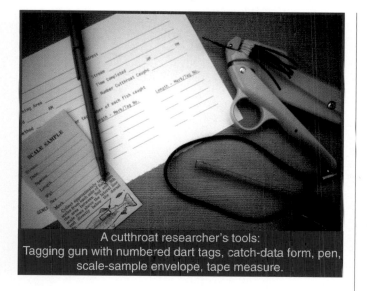

A cutthroat researcher's tools:
Tagging gun with numbered dart tags, catch-data form, pen, scale-sample envelope, tape measure.

more widespread in Oregon than in other states, and this has undoubtedly been a contributing factor (hatchery cutthroat have been stocked in virtually every large Oregon coastal stream at one time or another, but with the exception of the Siletz and Alsea systems, most of these programs have now been abandoned). Other problems include too-generous bag limits, the historic absence of regulations designed to protect smolts or downstream kelts, and the introduction of many exotic species.

All this, of course, is hindsight. Management efforts now focus on measures designed to conserve existing remnant populations and restore others. These include termination of hatchery programs, more restrictive regulations, more intensive population monitoring, and habitat-restoration programs. But the upshot is that it will be a long time, if ever, before Oregon anglers again enjoy the type of estuary angling for sea-run cutthroat that was once available to them.

Washington

Fisheries managers have divided Western Washington into five regions based on similarities in the life histories of their salmonid populations. Those regions, and what is currently known of their sea-run cutthroat populations, are as follows:

Lower Columbia River and Tributaries

Cutthroat stocks are generally depressed throughout this region. Angling censuses and counts of cutthroat returning to the Kalama River, an important Lower Columbia tributary, both show steady declines. As noted before, cutthroat stocks in the Wind and Klickitat Rivers already are believed extinct.

South Coast

This area is characterized by medium to large streams and early-entering sea-run cutthroat stocks. In Bingham Creek, a tributary of the Satsop and Chehalis Rivers which flow into the Grays Harbor estuary, numbers of outmigrating cutthroat smolts have remained constant from 1982 through 1994, although the size of the population before 1982 is unknown. Numbers of steelhead and coho smolts were both down over the same period. The Bingham

Creek cutthroat population apparently is holding its own, but the state has little or no information about other cutthroat stocks in this area. Angling reports suggest that the sea-run cutthroat population of Willapa Bay and its many tributary streams, once estimated at more than 100,000 fish, has declined precipitously.

North Coast

This area is characterized by small to large rivers flowing directly into the ocean and by early-entering cutthroat populations with older and larger smolts than stocks in most other regions. The state has no recent information on the health of these stocks.

South Puget Sound, Hood Canal, and the Strait of Juan de Fuca

This region is characterized by sheltered marine waters, smaller streams, and late-entering cutthroat populations. A research station on Big Beef Creek, which flows into Hood Canal, has kept records of cutthroat smolt migration since 1978. These have remained fairly constant and have even shown an increasing trend in recent years, but the number of smolts never has exceeded 1,000 even in the best years. The number of steelhead smolts also has remained consistent throughout the same period, while coho smolt numbers have trended downward.

Aside from Big Beef Creek, the state has little recent reliable information on the overall health of the area's cutthroat stocks, but some are believed healthy and others depressed.

North Puget Sound

Several large river systems flow into North Puget Sound and cutthroat tend to return to these rivers early, in August and September. Returning stocks usually include many immature fish (those not yet ready to spawn). Based on angling results and other data, cutthroat populations in this area are thought to be abundant and widespread. One biologist has estimated the cutthroat population of the Skagit system may be as high as 20,000 fish, and that of the neighboring Stillaguamish system perhaps 10,000. Extensive data on smolt migrations have been collected from this area, but had not been analyzed at this writing.

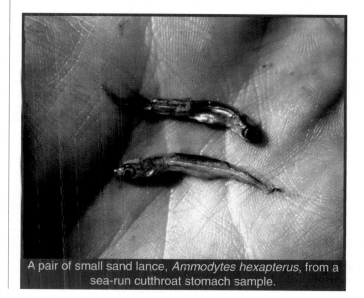

A pair of small sand lance, *Ammodytes hexapterus*, from a sea-run cutthroat stomach sample.

Washington has relied less on hatchery programs than Oregon, and now hatchery cutthroat are being planted only in the Lower Columbia and South Coast regions. Brief hatchery programs on the North Sound and North Coast and a more extensive program (1982 to 1992) in South Puget Sound have been discontinued. Even when these programs were at their peak, about 1986, fewer than 120,000 cutthroat were released in South Puget Sound, and in most years the number was much smaller. In addition to the hatchery programs, the state authorized at least one angling group to plant cutthroat eggs in Vibert boxes (slotted plastic boxes designed to protect eggs during development) placed in a stream flowing into Hood Canal. The eggs came from a hatchery, so in effect this was an extension of the state's hatchery program. This small-scale effort also has been discontinued.

In Lower Columbia tributaries, especially the Cowlitz River, where a very successful sea-run cutthroat fishery has been established, a total of about 250,000 hatchery cutthroat were released in 1993. Of that figure, nearly 150,000 fish went into the Cowlitz, another 42,400 into the Elochoman River, and 39,000 into the Washougal. Other major plants were made in the North Fork of the Lewis (21,600); the Coweeman River (15,900); Hoquiam River (13,900); Salmon Creek near Vancouver (10,700); and the Wishkah River (9,000). Wild cutthroat release regulations are in effect in areas where marked hatchery fish have been planted.

In an effort to assure that more cutthroat would survive to spawn at least once, the state several years ago imposed a minimum size limit of 14 inches and a daily bag limit of two fish in most areas inhabited by sea-runs. Since then, numbers of large cutthroat and spawning fish have both increased, especially in North and South Puget Sound and Hood Canal.

At the time this was written, the state was inventorying its salmonid populations to try to make up for an appalling lack of information, especially concerning sea-run cutthroat. State officials considered implementing a cutthroat punch-card system, similar to one that exists for steelhead, as a means of obtaining information about sea-runs, but ultimately rejected the idea because "there is already too much paperwork required in licensing anglers." Without such information, it is difficult to understand how an accu-

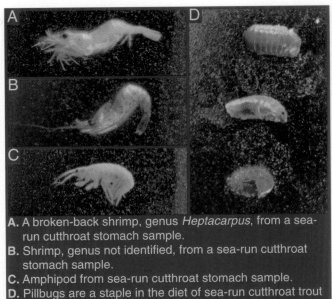

A. A broken-back shrimp, genus *Heptacarpus*, from a sea-run cutthroat stomach sample.
B. Shrimp, genus not identified, from a sea-run cutthroat stomach sample.
C. Amphipod from sea-run cutthroat stomach sample.
D. Pillbugs are a staple in the diet of sea-run cutthroat trout in estuaries. These are from a trout stomach sample.

rate assessment of stocks can be made. Not only that, but fisheries managers candidly admit that no matter what their inventory shows, salmon and steelhead, as more glamorous and commercially valuable species, will undoubtedly continue to receive more attention—and more money—than sea-run cutthroat.

The state is not alone in trying to find out more about sea-run populations. The Sea-Run Cutthroat Coalition, an organization of angling groups dedicated to sea-run cutthroat preservation and research, is engaged in its own stream-sampling and angler-survey programs in an effort to obtain more reliable information on the status of sea-run stocks. The coalition also is working to establish the first comprehensive data base of information on sea-run cutthroat. Such information exists in many journals and published or unpublished management reports, but is widely scattered and very difficult for biologists to access. The coalition hopes to identify all these different sources and assemble them in a computer data base that will be accessible to fisheries managers and biologists everywhere.

If some of Washington's sea-run cutthroat populations are still healthy, as managers suppose, it is probably more a result of good luck than good management. Unquestionably, though, some excellent fishing for sea-runs does remain, especially in the estuaries of North and South Puget Sound and Hood Canal, and with the efforts now under way by the state and volunteer groups such as the Sea-Run Cutthroat Coalition, there is at least some reason to hope this will continue to be the case.

British Columbia

About 1,000 streams flowing into the ocean have been identified along the British Columbia coast and its offshore islands. That may seem a small number for such a vast territory, but under the classification system used by the province the entire Fraser River drainage, with all its tributaries, was counted as only a single stream, so the reality is that while only 1,000 streams drain directly into salt water, those streams have a huge number of tributaries.

A total of 612 stocks of anadromous cutthroat have

The three-spined stickleback, *Gasterosteus aculaetus*, is a favorite seasonal food of sea-run cutthroat. It must hurt to swallow one of these, but they do it anyway.

been identified in these streams, but the province has information on the status of only 120 of these, mostly on the Lower Mainland or the eastern shore of Vancouver Island. Even for those areas, much of the information is anecdotal, what biologists call "soft" data, and there is virtually no information on the historic size of stocks.

Based on these "soft" data, biologists believe 15 stocks are now extinct (the real number probably is somewhat higher), 16 others are at high risk of extinction, 5 are at "moderate risk," and 30 are of "special concern." Fifty-four others are unthreatened, meaning the population is stable and under no great risk. The province has no information on the status of the 492 other cutthroat stocks known to exist in British Columbia.

The 15 populations believed extinct all were from small streams on the east coast of Vancouver Island or the Vancouver urban area. Biologists suspect other urban-area stocks probably are extinct, but lack information to verify this. Where extinction has occurred it was due to all the usual causes, with savage logging practices having been particularly at fault along the mainland coast and on Vancouver Island, while agricultural practices and rapid urbanization were the main culprits in the Lower Fraser Valley.

Most of the cutthroat stocks about which nothing is known are scattered along the North Coast of the province. Many of these are in isolated areas, far from human settlements of any size, so they should remain free from the effects of urbanization or agricultural practices for many years to come. But their isolation may not be enough to protect all of them from the impacts of logging or mining. New provincial forest-practices regulations require more consideration of fisheries habitat, but in B.C., as elsewhere, such regulations are only as good as the enforcement behind them—and the province has yet to establish a track record on that score.

British Columbia has initiated an urban stream-restoration program on the Lower Mainland and Vancouver Island, and habitat-restoration projects have been undertaken in other areas, primarily on Vancouver Island and in the Skeena River watershed. These projects typically involve placement of in-stream structures, mostly boulders, gravel, woody debris, or rip-rap. Follow-up surveys to

Author prepares to release the fish, which took a dry fly.

determine their success rate judged 55 percent of them "successful" or "outstanding" from a physical standpoint and 49 percent from a biological standpoint three years after completion. The percentage of outright failures was low in both cases. But lest anyone feel those figures are cause for celebration, consider this: What private business could survive if its products were successful only half the time? It appears there is much still to be learned about successful habitat restoration.

For the present, the status of most of British Columbia's sea-run cutthroat populations remains a mystery. Considering their relative isolation, however, it seems likely many are probably still untouched by anglers and relatively unaffected by other human activities. One can only hope that will continue to be the case until we learn more about their size, their health, and how to manage them properly.

Alaska

Cutthroat trout are the most abundant trout species in Southeast Alaska, and as such they are very important to anglers. North of the Alaska Panhandle their numbers taper off gradually to the limit of the cutthroat's range in Prince William Sound. As we have seen, sea-runs in Southeast Alaska are believed to overwinter in lakes, then return to salt water after ice-out in the spring and migrate to their spawning and rearing streams. Smolts are usually three years old and may make two winter migrations before spawning for the first time. Cutthroat in this region tend to live longer than others, with some individuals reaching 10 years of age.

Cutthroat angling harvest trends in Alaska have been generally downward from 1977 to 1993, but these figures include all types of cutthroat, resident as well as sea-run. In 1994, 22 percent of all cutthroat caught were taken from salt water, but other sea-runs undoubtedly were among the 78 percent caught in fresh water. The largest saltwater catch was in the Petersburg/Wrangell area of Southeast Alaska. Figures show that Alaskan anglers are releasing more and more fish, but angling effort is increasing concurrently.

As with most other jurisdictions, the State of Alaska has good information about only a few of its sea-run cutthroat stocks. The best information is from Lake Eva on Baranof Island and Auke Lake near Juneau, where biologists have

Author plays a sea-run cutthroat hooked in somebody's front yard on Hood Canal.

tracked cutthroat populations for a number of years. These efforts indicate recent increases in both populations; the number of outmigrants from Lake Eva was nearly twice as large in 1995 as in 1962-1964, and the Auke Lake outmigration also was up in 1994-95 over the early 1980s, including both hatchery and wild fish (hatchery fish are no longer being planted). But there are no data on the historic size of these runs.

The average number of outmigrant smolts from other systems is generally less than 1,000 fish, an indication of small cutthroat populations in general. The abundance of cutthroat in mixed-stock overwintering sites—that is, lakes where cutthroat from several different stocks mingle during the winter—also is low. The state lacks information from stream systems affected by logging or urban development and thus has no way of knowing the fate of native cutthroat populations in the Tongass National Forest near Ketchikan, which has been logged savagely in recent years.

In 1994 Alaska imposed new regulations designed to protect its cutthroat populations. These included a 12-inch minimum size limit overall, with 14 inches in "high-use" areas, and a ban on bait 10 months of the year. A two-fish bag and possession limit was established in Southeast Alaska, and a spring spawning closure and bait ban was imposed in Prince William Sound.

Steelhead

The winter-run steelhead, *Oncorhynchus mykiss*, sometimes offers spectacular fly fishing in the estuaries, but this type of fishing remains largely unknown because the conditions necessary for it do not occur very often.

Steelhead spawn in late winter or early spring and their eggs hatch in April, May, or later. Young steelhead usually spend at least a year feeding and growing in their native streams before smolting; those hatched in the rivers of Northern Californian and Oregon often smolt after only one year in fresh water, while steelhead hatched in rivers farther north usually require two or three years of freshwater life before smolting. There also appears to be a rough correlation between the time steelhead spend in fresh water and at sea; a fish that smolts after a single year often returns to spawn after only one year at sea, while a fish

that smolts after two years usually spends two years at sea before returning to spawn, and so on. There are exceptions, but this correlation accounts for the larger average size of adult steelhead throughout the northern part of their range; these fish spend more time in the rivers and more time at sea, and hence grow to large size.

Adult steelhead run in every month of the year, although from late spring through early fall they usually come to the rivers in small, scattered groups, and their small numbers and sporadic timing makes it very difficult for anglers to find them in the estuaries. Winter, however, is a different story. Beginning in late November or early December, winter-run steelhead return to the rivers of Washington and British Columbia in large numbers, usually in bursts or pulses; in many instances, these continue at intervals through March and April. The relatively large numbers of these fish and the fairly dependable timing of their returns sometimes makes it possible for anglers to intercept them in the estuaries. But favorable conditions, such as a lengthy spell of dry weather and a succession of low tides, do not occur very frequently. When they do occur, however, the fishing can be truly spectacular; the steelhead usually are in prime condition, as strong and bright as they will ever be, and often fight with twice the vigor and endurance of fish hooked in fresh water.

The best fishing is in small, protected estuaries, simply because it is much easier to find the fish in such confined waters. Fortunately, winter steelhead are not very picky about where they spawn, and there are runs in the smallest streams as well as the largest rivers. Scores of little winter-run steelhead streams drain into small estuaries in Puget Sound and Hood Canal; hundreds more may be found along the east coast of Vancouver Island or farther north along the Inside Passage. Southeast Alaska also has many little streams and estuaries, and similar fishing undoubtedly is available there in April and May, when the largest steelhead runs occur.

The less protected estuaries of the Oregon and Northern California coasts offer fewer opportunities for this type of fishing, but enterprising anglers willing to invest the time and effort to explore the possibilities could be well rewarded. More about this in a later chapter.

Sea-Run Dolly Varden

The Dolly Varden char, *Salvelinus malma*, offers more consistent and widespread opportunities for estuary fishing than the steelhead, but the Dolly Varden has never been as popular among anglers. Partly this is due to a perception that it does not fight as well as steelhead, cutthroat, or salmon, partly because it is considered something less than an ideal table fish. The Dolly Varden also has never outlived its reputation as a ruthless predator, vacuuming river bottoms for trout and salmon eggs and feeding voraciously on their newly hatched fry. Notwithstanding that Dolly Varden, steelhead, and salmon all managed to coexist and thrive for ages before the white man's arrival, some of the region's settlers took it upon themselves to stamp out the Dolly Varden so it could no longer exercise its predatory ways. As a consequence, Dollies became targets of an extermination campaign that lasted many years, and the success of these efforts can still be measured by the relative scarcity of these fish throughout the southern part of their range.

Southeast Alaska has countless small estuaries where salmon, steelhead, cutthroat, and Dolly Varden come and go.

A silvery bright sea-run Dolly Varden, taken on a dry fly in the estuary of Peterson Creek, Alaska.

Despite its reputation and relative scarcity in some areas, there are still anglers who enjoy fishing for Dollies. Most such fishing takes place in rivers, but the Dolly is unquestionably at its best as a sea-run fish and is seasonally available in estuaries, especially in Southeast Alaska and other parts of its northern range.

Dolly Varden spawn in late summer or early fall; after spawning, some return immediately to salt water while others remain in the rivers over winter. The latter, along with outmigrating smolts, enter the estuaries from late spring through early summer. Young fish feed close to shore, mostly on amphipods and shrimp, while adults range into deeper, open waters, sometimes traveling 100 miles or more from their rivers of origin, and pursue forage species such as capelin, herring, and sand eels. Recent studies indicate that while large Dolly Varden do eat salmon fry in rivers, they rarely seek them in salt water, even when fry are abundant—further proof, if any were needed, that their reputation as predators is exaggerated.

It is usually during these spring feeding forays in the estuaries that Dolly Varden become available to anglers. Once they enter salt water they quickly assume the typical appearance and trappings of sea-run fish, becoming bright silver along their flanks. The pink and yellow spots that were instrumental in the naming of the fish (the name is derived from a colorful hat worn by Dolly Varden, a character in Dickens' novel *Barnaby Rudge*) fade to the point that one must look closely to see them at all. Indeed, a well-conditioned sea-run Dolly looks so bright and trout-like than an angler may have to look carefully to tell what he or she has caught.

Mature sea-run Dollies may still be a little on the lean side if caught early in the season, but they fatten up quickly and give a better account of themselves when hooked on a fly in estuarine waters than at any other stage of their lives. That is not to say they will make an angler forget salmon or steelhead, but neither are they to be casually dismissed. They lack the endurance of other salmonids, but their fight is stubborn while it lasts and sometimes they come to the surface and thrash about, although I have never seen one jump completely out of the water.

There are not many fisheries where sea-run Dolly Varden are specifically targeted, but one such is in the estuary of the Skagit River in Washington State. Even in this case, it's debatable whether Dollies or sea-run cutthroat are the primary target, but many Dollies are caught in this fishery, which usually is best in April. Doubtless Dolly Varden are taken elsewhere by other anglers, especially in the estuaries of Southeast Alaska where they are most abundant, but in these fisheries, too, they may be only secondary targets. Nevertheless, the Dolly Varden has its own rightful place in the spectrum of anadromous salmonids and provides another opportunity for estuary fly fishers.

Unlike most anadromous species, which come and go seasonally, marine gamefish are nearly always present in the estuaries. Nevertheless, they have always ranked well below the anadromous salmonids in the esteem of anglers, particularly fly fishers. In view of their low-visibility lifestyle, this is hardly surprising; they tend to be deeper-ranging fish than salmonids, not so easily seen or caught by fly fishers, and they do not fight as spectacularly, rarely surfacing until they are too tired to resist any longer. For these reasons, anglers have been slow to explore or exploit the potential of these fish.

Yet some species have achieved more popularity than others, and for good reason. The sea perch and rockfish are the most prominent of these; while neither jumps like a salmon or a trout, both are excellent sport fish in their own right, and both are relatively accessible to fly fishers.

Sea Perch

Also known as surf perch, the sea perch of the family *Embiotocidae* are among the few fish that bear fully developed live young. This was first noted in 1853 when an angler named A.C. Jackson caught some black surf perch in San Francisco Bay, placed them in a bucket of water, then noticed with great surprise that one of them appeared to be giving birth to miniature copies of itself. Recognizing this as very unusual behavior for a fish, Jackson notified authorities of his discovery, which eventually was reported to the naturalist Louis Agassiz at Harvard University. Agassiz studied the fish, confirmed that females did indeed carry embryos in their ovaries and bore them as fully developed live young, and conferred the name *Embiotocidae* on the sea perch family in recognition of this behavior. The black surf perch itself was named *Embiotoca jacksoni*, in Jackson's honor.

Twenty-three species of sea perch are known, and 21 of these inhabit the Pacific Coast of North America; the others are found in the waters of Korea and the Sea of Japan. Of the species indigenous to North American waters, one is a freshwater fish, the tule perch, which inhabits the Russian and Sacramento River systems in California. All the others are strictly marine in character, occupying a variety of environments, from the wild, turbulent surf along the Pacific shore (hence the popular name surf perch), to the calm, protected waters of coastal bays and inlets.

The surf-dwellers, which include the barred surf perch, *Amphistichus argenteus*, and redtail surf perch, *Amphistichus rhodoterus*, are the most familiar to sport fishermen, who seek them along the ocean beaches of Oregon, California, and Washington. Of more interest to estuary anglers are those species inhabiting calmer waters, although a few species appear to be at home in either calm water or turbulent surf.

The striped sea perch, *Embiotoca lateralis*, is probably the most important of the estuarial species. One reason is its size; it reaches lengths of 15 inches and weights of two pounds or more, which makes it one of the largest of the quiet-water sea perch. Another is its range, which extends all the way from Southeast Alaska to Baja California. The striped sea perch also is by far the most attractive member of the family; like all sea perch, it has a compressed body, exaggerated oblate shape, and sharply forked tail, but what sets it apart from all others is its color. Young stripers are a bright golden color, but as they grow older this fades to a sort of salmon-orange or copper hue marked with iridescent cobalt-blue horizontal stripes extending from head to tail. A mature striped sea perch surely is one of the most beautiful fish to be found in Northwest estuaries.

Along with its other virtues, the striped sea perch takes flies readily and is a hard, stubborn fighter. Often it is difficult for an angler to tell immediately whether he or she has hooked a sea perch or a sea-run cutthroat, for both fight similarly; about the only difference is that sea perch never come to the surface of their own free will. Striped sea perch also are excellent table fish, and they are among the few

A pair of striped sea perch and a starry flounder, all taken on a shrimp imitation in a shallow Puget Sound estuary.

species that seem able to make the transition from quiet water to the noisy, chaotic world of the surf, although they are most often found in sheltered bays, inlets, and estuaries.

As with all male sea perch, striper males have a gland near the anal fin that is used in copulation with females. During mating, the female continues swimming in its normal upright or vertical position while the male maneuvers horizontally until the genital organs of both fish come in contact; actual copulation takes place in only a few seconds. Fertilized eggs in the female develop into embryos that are carried and nurtured in the ovaries. The number of embryos is related to the age and size of the fish; studies have shown that a female striped sea perch reproducing for the first time—normally at age three—carries an average of 18 embryos; this will increase to an average of 32 by the time the fish reaches seven years of age.

The embryos are nourished by the ovarian fluid until fully developed. Birth usually takes place in June or July in northern waters. Young fish are subject to predation by other fish, including other species of sea perch, and tend to seek refuge in kelp forests, where they also begin feeding. Other feeding habitats include eelgrass beds, rocky reefs, and beaches.

Striped sea perch are carnivorous fish that seek their food visually; they forage in water less than 20 feet deep, often much shallower, and this places them within easy reach of fly fishers. Since they move about in densely packed schools, an angler who catches one can usually expect to catch many more.

Striped sea perch have slightly larger mouths than most of the quiet-water sea perch, which allow them a somewhat more varied diet. Scud-like amphipods make up the bulk of their food, but they also feed heavily on isopods, shrimp, crabs, and polychaete worms. They also are known to eat snails, mussels, and barnacles, although that knowledge is not much help to fly fishers.

Growth of both male and female fish is rapid throughout the first three or four years of life; thereafter males grow more slowly while females continue growing at the same rate. The largest striped sea perch are therefore likely to be females, a matter of importance when a decision must be made whether to keep or release a fish.

Old pilings are likely spots for sea perch and cutthroat. These are the remains of an old ferry dock on Puget Sound.

The pile sea perch, *Rhacochilus vacca*, is another important target for estuarine anglers. Its range is similar to that of the striped sea perch, but its common name stems from its habit of congregating around pilings, especially those driven into cobbled or rocky bottoms, although it also is occasionally found in open waters. In Puget Sound it is sometimes called the dusky sea perch.

The pile perch reaches sizes even larger than the striped sea perch, attaining a maximum length of 17 1/2 inches and weights of more than three pounds. Mostly bright silver in color, it has a large dark bar on either flank behind the pectoral fin, usually trending in a diagonal direction. The front of the soft-rayed portion of its dorsal fin rises to a peak, extending above the spines in front and the other rays in back.

Like all sea perch, pile perch bear live young, although their mating behavior is slightly different from that of the striped sea perch; both male and female pile perch swim horizontally or even upside down while mating. Fecundity of females also varies, from an average of 11.7 embryos in females reproducing for the first time, usually at age four, to an average of more than 60 in females from seven to ten years old. Live birth occurs during August in northern waters.

While there are many similarities in the life histories and physical characteristics of pile perch and sea perch, there are also some significant differences. Pile perch, for unknown reasons, appear to migrate into deeper water during winter months, so their availability to estuary anglers is limited to a period extending from about May or June through November. Pile perch also have well-developed fused tooth plates in their mouths which makes it possible for them to crush hard-shelled animals, and this characteristic has prompted some taxonomists to argue they should be classified in the genus *Damalichthys* rather than *Rhacochilus*. The taxonomic debate means little to anglers, but the feeding habits associated with these specialized pharyngeal tooth plates are important; pile perch like to eat things that are very hard for fly fishers to imitate, such as snails, mussels, barnacles, brittle stars, clams, and sometimes sea urchins. The fact that some of these organisms, especially mussels and barnacles, grow in thick clusters on pilings may explain the pile perch's habit of swarming around such structures.

The good news for fly fishers is that pile perch also sometimes feed on amphipods and crabs and will take imitations of both; I have also taken them on baitfish imitations, although forage fish are not known to be a regular part of their diet. Like striped sea perch, they often move about in dense schools, but—perhaps because of their usual preference for fixed or slow-moving hard-shelled creatures—they are not as easily taken on flies. When they are hooked, their fighting behavior is similar to that of the striped sea perch.

The other sea perch most likely to be encountered by estuary fly fishers is the little shiner perch, *Cymatogaster aggregata*. Growing to a maximum length of only about seven inches, it is too small to be worth the attention of serious anglers, but it makes an excellent quarry for children just learning to fish. The range of this fish extends from Southeast Alaska to Northern Baja. It is typically bright silver in color with dark horizontal bars; male fish also have three vertical yellow bars on either flank.

The shiner perch occupies a wide variety of quiet-water habitats, from sandy-bottomed bays to eelgrass beds to pilings and piers. It also travels in schools.

At least two other species of sea perch are occasionally taken by anglers in Northwest estuaries; these are the white sea perch, *Phanerodon furcastus,* and the kelp perch, *Brachyistius frenatus*, both much less common than the species already mentioned.

The white sea perch may reach lengths of 12 inches, but usually is much smaller; it is similar in appearance to the pile perch except that it has a distinct black stripe extending along the base of the dorsal fin and lacks the single dark diagonal bar that the pile perch has on either flank. While sometimes found in loosely packed schools in shallow water, it tends to range in deeper waters than either the pile perch or striped sea perch.

The kelp perch, as its name indicates, spends most of its time in and around kelp beds. Even smaller than the white sea perch, rarely exceeding eight inches in length, it can hardly be considered an important sport fish and is mentioned here only because it may occasionally be encountered by fly fishers in pursuit of other species. The kelp perch is copper-orange in color and sometimes has small black spots along its lateral line. It feeds on small crustaceans living in kelp forests.

The black sea perch, *E. jacksoni*, which already has been mentioned, is available to anglers fishing California estuaries. The habits and life history of the black sea perch are very similar to those of the striped sea perch, and the two may sometimes be found in competition with one another for the same food stocks in the same waters. The black sea perch also reaches sizes similar to the striped sea perch, which makes it a worthwhile target for anglers. Its range extends from San Francisco Bay to Central Baja. It exhibits a wide variety of coloration, both dark and light, and the most reliable means of identification is a band of enlarged scales between the pectoral and ventral fins.

Sea perch have been fished commercially in some locations, particularly in California waters, but little serious effort has been made to monitor the status of sea perch stocks throughout most of their range. This is unfortunate, for it has led to the decline of some stocks. The once numerous populations of striped sea perch and pile sea perch in Puget Sound are an example; both stocks have declined sharply in recent years, victims of virtually unregulated commercial, recreational, and personal-use fisheries. Moreover, since these fish do not rank very high on the scale of commercial value, especially in northern waters, it seems improbable they will receive the attention they deserve from fisheries managers.

Rockfish

Members of the family *Scorpaenidae* and the genus *Sebastes*, rockfish receive their common name from their preference for rocky habitats, either high- or low-relief rocky reefs, generally in deeper water. In the parlance of biologists, they are known as "sedentary" fish, meaning they do not migrate but stay pretty close to home. Several experiments, however, have demonstrated that when removed from familiar habitats they are able to find their way back, so long as they are not released too far away.

About 100 species of rockfish have been identified, making *Sebastes* the single largest genus found along the Pacific Coast of North America, and many different specialized adaptive behaviors are represented among this large variety. All rockfish are bass-like in shape, but they display many variations in color; some of these are suggested by their common names, which include the copper, brown, black, black-and-yellow, redbanded, tiger, calico, canary, aurora, vermilion, blue, rosy, and olive rockfish. Along with these differences in color they also display many schemes of spots, stripes, blotches, or mottling. It is always risky to make generalizations about fish, particularly a genus like *Sebastes* with so many different species, but perhaps it is safe to say that among the rockfish the deeper-dwelling species tend more to be red or orange in color while those found in shallower water are more often shades of brown, green, or black.

The spines of the ventral, anal, and dorsal fins in rockfish (especially the dorsal) are sharp and mildly venomous to humans, and a puncture wound can cause swelling, redness and pain similar to that caused by a local infection, so these fish should always be handled with care.

As with sea perch, female rockfish are fertilized internally by males. The eggs hatch and are carried internally as embryos by the females, but not until they are fully developed; instead, they are ejected as living embryos that must develop further on their own. This reproductive strategy allows a female rockfish to nourish and expel an enormous number of embryos.

Rockfish provide important commercial and sport fisheries all along the West Coast of the United States and Canada; those taken in the commercial catch are commonly sold in fish markets under false names, such as snapper, sea bass, ocean perch or cod, apparently under the theory that the name "rockfish" is not appealing to the human appetite.

The majority of rockfish species inhabit water so deep they are well beyond the reach of fly fishers, but some are found in shallower inlets, bays, and estuaries. Even in these waters, however, they often spend most of their time in deep water during daylight hours and come within reach of fly fishers only during twilight or darkness. There are reports of rockfish feeding on the surface for schools of baitfish or floating crab larvae during daylight hours, but this apparently does not happen with regularity.

While more than two dozen species of rockfish are found in Puget Sound, Hood Canal, the Strait of Juan de Fuca, and the straits and bays of the Inside Passage of British Columbia and Southeast Alaska, the two species probably most often captured by fly fishers are the copper rockfish, *S. caurinus*, and the quillback rockfish, *S. maliger*. The range of these two species extends from Alaska to Baja California. Another species, the brown rockfish, *S. auriculatus*, also is commonly encountered in central and southern Puget Sound; its range extends from Alaska to mid-California. All three species display variations in color, so identification may be somewhat difficult, but the copper rockfish usually has a white or light-colored stripe following its lateral line, often with dark brown or brownish-green mottling along the back; the quillback is noted for its unusually high and deeply notched dorsal spines and dark brown color overlaid with

Pilings in the mist.

yellow and orange blotches; and the brown rockfish usually is distinguished by a dark spot on its upper gill cover, almost like a "false eye;" otherwise it is mostly dark brown with pink fins.

All three species prefer rocky reefs or holes in water less than 90 feet deep; they also are fond of artificial reefs, and once these are put in place they are usually colonized by rockfish within a matter of weeks. Copper, quillback, and brown rockfish may exceed 20 inches in length and 10 pounds in weight, although the average size is much smaller. They are very tough, determined fighters, and a heavy rockfish hooked in or near a kelp forest is often more than a match for a middle-weight fly rod.

Female rockfish release their embryos during the spring in northern waters. Little is known of the final stages of embryonic development, but it is likely the young fish shelter beneath layers of kelp or other algae or in eelgrass beds to escape predation. Here they remain as juveniles until they are large and mobile enough to range into deeper water without becoming easy targets for larger predators. Growth is rapid, with young fish reaching lengths of three or four inches within six months of birth. Thereafter the growth rate slows drastically, however, and it may take a rockfish from five to ten years to reach maturity and a weight of three or four pounds.

Copper, quillback, and brown rockfish have a tendency to congregate over high-relief rocky reefs or rock piles during the winter and move into shallower water during the summer, when they are often found over low-relief reefs or in eelgrass beds or kelp forests, especially in areas featuring both reefs and kelp. They display a marked preference for the bull kelp *Nereocystis leutkeana*, and fisheries biologists have theorized that floating gardens of kelp provide food, shelter, and spawning-release sites. When the kelp dies back in the fall, rockfish move back to reefs in deeper water and remain there over winter, apparently confining their foraging to very small areas. They are carnivorous and prey mostly on small fish, possibly including smaller fish of their own kind, as well as small sea perch. Other forage species include sculpin, blennies, shrimp, crabs, clams, and worms. Their seasonal and diurnal movements expose them to estuary fly fishers mostly during hours of twilight and darkness during the summer months; at these times they may be caught along rock jetties, sea walls, or kelp beds.

The black rockfish, *S. melanops*, probably is the most familiar species to coastal anglers from British Columbia to Southern California—certainly it is the species most often encountered in Oregon waters—but it is usually taken in the ocean, not in shallower estuaries. Other common species, sometimes found in estuaries, include the blue rockfish, *S. mysiinus*; yellowtail rockfish, *S. flavidus*; and tiger rockfish, *S. nigrocinctus*.

Even though rockfish have commercial value, there

has not been enough attention paid to the health of various stocks. Twenty-five years ago, rockfish were common in Puget Sound and could even be caught from sea walls and jetties in the Seattle metropolitan area; now they are rarely encountered by anglers. It seems likely their decline has been due to a rapacious commercial fishery, either targeting rockfish specifically or taking them as part of the "incidental bycatch" while fishing for other species. This was allowed to happen without significant interference or regulation by state fisheries managers—an all-too-common problem, and unfortunately one not confined to Washington State.

Other Marine Species

After sea perch and rockfish, it's a long distance to the next fish on the popularity list of marine species sought by estuary fly fishers. There is also considerable doubt about what the next fish should be, for while sea perch and rockfish are sometimes intentional angling targets—in other words, people fish purposefully for them—other marine species are most often caught incidentally by anglers fishing for something else.

There are exceptions to this. Some years ago there was a brief flurry of interest in fly fishing for Pacific cod, *Gadus macrocephalus*. This species, abundant in northern waters, ordinarily is found at considerable depths, but there is a late winter spawning migration into the shallower waters of Puget Sound and the Inside Passage, and Pacific cod may be taken on a fly in these waters from late winter to midsummer. They prefer rocky bottoms in less than ten feet of water, but are also caught from piers, usually during late twilight or darkness. Sometimes the best fishing is from piers equipped with electric lights, which seem to attract cod at night.

Pacific cod grow to more than three feet in length, but those taken by estuary anglers usually are much smaller, averaging three or four pounds; apparently, only the smaller individuals are willing to come into water shallow enough to be easily caught with a fly. Like most bottomfish, they fight stubbornly but not spectacularly. The brief interest in these fish, back in the late 1970s, led some fly anglers to target them specifically, but after a year or two the interest seemed to ebb. Since then, Pacific cod have joined the growing list of victims of intensive commercial fishing and have become scarce in Puget Sound.

The walleye pollack, *Theragra chalcogramma*, is a member of the same family as the Pacific cod and also enters shallower waters during the winter. I have heard of some instances of pollack being taken on flies, but I do not believe there is yet enough sporting interest in this fish to elevate it to the status of a target species.

The starry flounder, *Platichthys stellatus*, is abundant

The late Enos Bradner fishing Dewatto Bay, Washington.

in estuaries, takes flies readily—some might say too readily—and is a reasonably good table fish, all of which would seem to make it a good candidate for popularity among anglers. Unfortunately, the starry flounder is almost without sporting qualities; it fights, if that is the right word, with all the liveliness and pep of an old hubcap. Probably it would fight better if it could, but a fish with the body shape and life history of the starry flounder definitely has limited options.

Any angler who fishes Pacific Coast estuaries with a wet fly is bound to hook a starry flounder sooner or later, so it is good to know something about these fish. The starry flounder is a member of the family *Pleuronectidae*, or right-eye flounders, all of which are distinguished by their flat, generally oblate shapes. However, the starry flounder is unique in that it is the only member of the family whose eyes and coloration may be on either the right *or* left side of its body (although they are on the right side in most cases).

Starry flounders spawn in late winter or early spring. Young fish swim in an upright position with eyes on either side of their head, but eventually choose to rest on either their right or left side. When they do so, the eye on the underside migrates until both eyes are positioned on the upper side of the head. This side also develops mottled black or brown spots over the broad flank of the fish and dark bars or bands on its fins; the underside remains cream or white.

In estuaries, starry flounder are usually found in shallow water over sandy bottoms. They bury themselves under a thin layer of sand so that only their eyes are showing; the sand and the matching colors of the fish provide perfect camouflage. Once buried, the fish waits for its prey, which may include crabs, shrimp, worms, clams, or even small fish. When startled, a starry flounder quickly takes flight, and these sudden departures are often visible to anglers as explosions of sand or silt on the bottom.

Large starry flounder prefer deep water and those found in estuaries are usually smaller individuals, up to 20 inches in length. They are sometimes even found in the tidal reaches of rivers flowing into estuaries.

Other members of the flounder family are taken occasionally by estuary fly fishers, especially the English sole, *Parophrys vetulus,* and the Pacific halibut, *Hippoglossus stenolepis,* more common in Alaskan waters than elsewhere.

The ling cod, *Ophiodon elongatus,* and the kelp greenling, *Hexagrammos decagrammus,* are also sometimes taken by fly fishers, usually those seeking rockfish around kelp beds or rock piles—the same type of habitat preferred by ling cod and greenling.

Ling cod are aggressive fish that grow to large size and feed on other fish, including rockfish, pollack, flounder, hake, and true cod. They are widely distributed along the Pacific Coast and are found in most large estuaries, from the surface to great depths. As with most marine species, the larger fish dwell mostly in deeper water, but fly fishers specifically targeting these fish and employing the proper techniques sometimes take ling cod in double-digit weights. The kelp greenling feeds on shrimp, small fish, and worms and does not reach sizes as large as the ling cod, but is perhaps more easily caught in shallow waters.

A winter snowstorm sweeps over an estuary on Hood Canal.

Members of the sculpin family, *Cottidae,* are ubiquitous in West Coast estuaries; at least 36 species have been recorded in Puget Sound alone. For the most part, they are more of an annoyance than a desirable gamefish, and anyone who fishes a wet fly will find that he or she can scarcely keep them off the hook. Not all these fish are considered annoyances, however; a few species even border on desirability.

The first member of the sculpin family an angler is likely to meet in the estuaries of the Pacific Northwest is the Pacific staghorn sculpin, *Leptocottus armatus,* an ugly little fish which, like most sculpin, has an enormous mouth in proportion to its size. The Pacific staghorn sculpin is most often found over muddy or sandy bottoms, where it sometimes buries itself up to its eyes, but occasionally it is found over rocky bottoms as well. It grows to a maximum length of 18 inches, but most specimens hooked by fly fishers—inevitably while fishing for some other species—are less than five inches long. They have no sporting value whatever, and the tough membrane in the staghorn sculpin's mouth sometimes makes it difficult to remove a fly.

Some members of the sculpin family reach much larger sizes, however, and these do provide some sport. Foremost is the cabezon, *Scorpaenichthys marmoratus,* which ranges all the way from Northern British Columbia to Baja California and may reach weights of 25 pounds. The name cabezon means "big head," and these fish—while definitely not handsome—are known as hard fighters. They are found anywhere from the intertidal zone to deep water, most often the latter, frequently around kelp beds where they are sometimes taken by anglers seeking rockfish. They feed almost exclusively on crabs.

There are probably other marine species with sporting qualities as yet undiscovered, and fly fishers, with their traditional preoccupation for anadromous salmonids, have barely explored the possibilities of taking these fish in the estuaries. Even for the fish listed here, whose sporting qualities already have been established, much remains to be done in determining the best times, places, tactics, and fly patterns. It would not be an exaggeration to say that this work represents one of the last unexplored frontiers of fly fishing.

Except when rivers flood, the pulse and rhythm of an estuary and all its life are controlled by the daily rise and fall of tides. The tide comes and goes as if driven by the slow, steady beat of a giant heart, flooding the far corners of the estuary with life-giving fluid in a mysterious, semi-regular rhythm geared to the celestial forces that hold the earth in its appointed place. Fish follow the tide, and the strength of its flow may determine whether they follow it with vigor, moving swiftly and feeding actively, or whether they follow it slowly and sullenly and without interest in whatever food it stirs. Anglers, too, must follow the tide, not only because it influences the behavior of the fish they seek, but also because it largely determines how and when they can fish, or even whether they can fish at all.

Knowledge of local tides is absolutely vital to the estuary fly fisher, yet most anglers understand tides poorly if at all. Ask the average fisherman how tides work and almost certainly you will receive an explanation that is either inaccurate, incomplete, or both. Even those few anglers who do understand the basic mechanics of the tides may not know how they vary by latitude or locale, or that Atlantic and Pacific Coast tides usually are of different types, or that the United States, Canada, and other nations use different benchmarks to measure tides.

It might be argued that estuary anglers have no need to know these things to fish their local waters, and that would be true; familiarity with local tides and their effects on fishing are the only requirements for success. Nevertheless, I have elected to give a relatively comprehensive explanation of tidal mechanics and the way tides are predicted, mainly because every other fishing book I have ever seen has given these subjects extremely short shrift and it seems well past time to correct the deficiency. Also, I like to know how and why things work, and if the reader shares that sort of curiosity, then the explanation will be of interest.

Tidal Mechanics

Tides are short-period, astronomically induced vertical changes in the local height of sea level. They are caused primarily by differences between the gravitational and centrifugal forces that hold the earth and moon in equilibrium; the sun plays a role in this, too, but of lesser importance than the moon.

The earth's own gravity holds the seas to its surface, but the gravity of both the sun and the moon are also constantly pulling on the earth, tugging at every atom on the planet, including its seas and atmosphere. If gravity were the only force at work, the earth and moon would have crashed into one another long ago, undoubtedly with unpleasant consequences for life on earth, but there is an equal and opposite force that keeps this from happening. This is the centrifugal force, a product of the earth's revolution around the common center of mass of the earth-moon system, and it exactly offsets the gravitational attraction between the earth and moon, keeping the two bodies in a state of equilibrium.

The centrifugal force is of equal magnitude at every point on the surface of the earth, and is always directed away from the moon. However, the magnitude of the gravitational force exerted by the moon varies at different points on earth because not all points on earth are the same distance from the moon. The resulting local difference between the moon's gravitational pull and the offsetting centrifugal force is known as the *tide-producing force*, and it accounts for the phenomenon of the tides.

These differences exist because the moon's gravitational pull is always stronger on one side of the earth than the other, simply because one side of the planet always is closer to the moon than the other. The pull of the moon's gravity on this side—the side facing the moon—is strong enough locally to exceed the opposing centrifugal force, and when that pull is exerted on the ocean, it results in an outward tidal "bulge" in the direction of the moon. This bulge is known as a *direct tide*. Simultaneously, on the opposite side of the earth, at the point farthest from the moon, the strength of the moon's gravity is locally weaker than the opposing centrifugal force, so the centrifugal force generates its own outward "bulge" of seawater facing away from the moon. This is known as an *opposite tide*.

Low tide reveals a sandbar not visible at high water. If you get stranded on one of these, your spouse might not buy the explanation when you get home late.

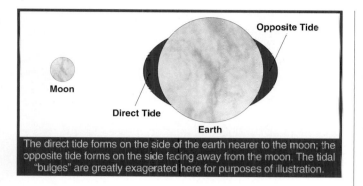

The direct tide forms on the side of the earth nearer to the moon; the opposite tide forms on the side facing away from the moon. The tidal "bulges" are greatly exagerated here for purposes of illustration.

As the earth rotates on its axis, a point on its surface may face first toward the moon and pass through the "bulge" created by its pull; later the same day, when the earth has completed half a rotation, the same point will reach opposition to the moon and encounter the "bulge" resulting from centrifugal force. Thus most places on earth experience two high tides a day.

Because we measure tides on a vertical scale we tend to think of these tidal bulges as places where the moon's gravity or the offsetting centrifugal force has caused water to be drawn up or pushed out in a vertical direction. But neither of these forces is strong enough to overcome the earth's own gravity in a vertical direction; what actually happens is that each force has a horizontal component that causes water to flow horizontally in the form of shallow-water waves known as *tidal currents* or "tidal waves" (not to be confused with earthquake-caused tsunami waves). These waves collect at the points of the direct and opposite tides, and the horizontal component that induces their movement is known as the *tractive force*.

As the earth rotates on its axis and the moon travels along in its orbit, the tidal waves or currents generated by the tractive force keep moving in response to the constantly changing points of strongest and weakest lunar gravitational influence. They are not able to keep pace in real time, however, because inertia, friction, the interplay between the gravitational forces of the sun and moon, and other factors act to speed them up or slow them down, so their arrival at a given point may be ahead of the moon's passage over the local meridian, or as much as several hours behind.

The passage of one of these traveling waves creates a local high tide, although on the open sea the difference in water height may be so small as to be scarcely measurable. That difference increases substantially, however, when a wave encounters the shallow water of a continental shelf, or when it strikes the land mass of the continent itself. The measured vertical rise in sea-level height in reference to a baseline measured at a given point on land is what we commonly think of as a high tide.

Because it takes 24 hours for the earth to complete a rotation on its axis, it would seem that successive high tides should always be 12 hours apart, even if they do lag behind the actual moment of maximum or minimum lunar gravitational influence. But the moon is moving, too, and in the time it takes for the earth to complete a single rotation, the moon advances a little more than 12 degrees in its orbit. Because of that advance, it requires more than a full 24 hours for a point on the earth's surface to "catch up" with the moon's new orbital position; the actual time required is about 24 hours and 50 minutes. Thus the time between suc-

cessive daily high waters averages 12 hours and 25 minutes; this also is the reason high tides occur approximately 50 minutes later every solar day.

The tractive force that causes water to flow horizontally and collect to form the "bulges" of the direct and opposite tides also causes stable depressions in the height of sea level at other points on the earth's surface. These depressions, always at right angles to a line drawn between the direct and opposite tides, represent low tides, and logically one would expect them also to occur twice daily at any given location at a time midway between successive high waters. In fact they do, but there are many variables and complexities that can and do influence both the time and height of local tides. Of these we will see more later.

The sun's gravitational pull also influences the tides, but because the sun is so much farther away from the earth than the moon, its influence is correspondingly weaker—at most, about 46 percent of the moon's—although in areas far from the equator, and thus farther away from the moon, the sun actually is the dominant force. In these areas successive tides occur 12 hours apart on the average, instead of 12 hours and 25 minutes.

Spring and Neap Tides

Twice each lunar month, at the time of the new and the full moon, the sun and moon come roughly into line with one another, an event with a marvelous name from the back pages of the dictionary: *syzygy*. When this happens, the gravitational forces of the sun and moon complement one another and are directed roughly at the same spot on earth. The result is an increase in the local difference between gravitational pull and centrifugal force, leading to a corresponding increase in the tractive force. This means high tides will be higher than normal and low tides will be lower. These events are called *spring tides*, although they occur each month and have nothing whatever to do with the season (the term actually comes from an Anglo-Saxon word meaning "to jump").

Conversely, when the sun and moon are at right angles to one another, as they are when the moon is in its first and last quarter, their gravitational pulls work at right angles on the earth and tend to cancel one another partly. The result is "flatter" tides—highs that are lower than usual, lows that are higher than usual. These are called *neap tides*, from a Greek word meaning 'scant." Thus the phases of the moon are of particular importance to estuary anglers because in large measure they determine what tides one may expect.

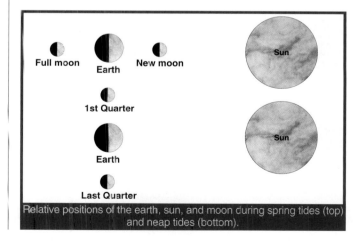

Relative positions of the earth, sun, and moon during spring tides (top) and neap tides (bottom).

A small estuary on Hood Canal, about an hour after morning high tide. At this stage there's plenty of water to launch a small boat and go fishing.

So far, so good. Now things get a little more complicated.

One complication is posed by the moon's orbit around the earth. Because it is an elliptical (oval) orbit, the moon's distance from the earth is constantly changing. During the 27.3 days it takes for the moon to complete a revolution in orbit, its distance from earth varies by as much as 31,000 miles, and as its distance varies, so does the moon's gravitational influence on earth. When the moon is closest to earth, its gravitational force is correspondingly greater and the tidal range—the vertical distance between high and low tide—is increased by about 20 percent; when it is farthest away from earth, the tidal range is reduced by about the same percentage.

The earth also is in an elliptical orbit, which means its distance varies from the sun. Its closest approach to the sun usually occurs January 2, and on that date the sun's gravitational pull has its greatest effect on earth's tides, with a corresponding increase in the tidal range. Earth's farthest retreat from the sun usually occurs July 2, and the tidal range accordingly is reduced then. But again, because the sun is so far away, the difference in tidal ranges resulting from these near and far approaches is smaller than those resulting from the advance and retreat of the moon.

Semidiurnal, Diurnal, and Mixed Tides

The moon's orbit around the earth also is inclined, or "tilted," about 5 degrees to the plane of the earth's orbit around the sun. Add to that the fact that the earth's equator is itself inclined about 23 1/2 degrees to the plane of the earth's orbit, and you will see that as the moon revolves around the earth it must cross over the equator twice each lunar month, spending half its time north of the equator and half to the south, ranging a maximum of 28 1/2 degrees in either direction.

When the moon crosses over the equator, the direct and opposite tides straddle the equatorial line; thus successive high and low tides are similar in height at any location and occur twice daily, spaced nearly equally in time. These are called *semidiurnal* tides.

But when the moon moves north or south of the equator, the direct tide forms in one hemisphere and the oppo-

site tide in the other. For example, if the moon is north of the equator, the direct tide will form in the Northern Hemisphere and the opposite tide will be in the Southern Hemisphere. As the earth rotates, a point in the Northern Hemisphere may pass through the bulges or "envelopes" of both the direct and opposite tides but they will be of different heights. A point on line "A" in the illustration, for example, will pass through the bulge of the direct tide at its maximum, but only through the thin outer edge of the bulge created by the opposite tide. Thus such a point will experience twice daily high tides of unequal height; these are known as *mixed* tides.

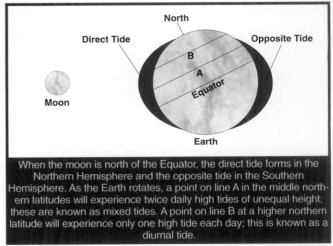

When the moon is north of the Equator, the direct tide forms in the Northern Hemisphere and the opposite tide in the Southern Hemisphere. As the Earth rotates, a point on line A in the middle northern latitudes will experience twice daily high tides of unequal height; these are known as mixed tides. A point on line B at a higher northern latitude will experience only one high tide each day; this is known as a diurnal tide.

Even farther north, a location on line "B" in the illustration will pass through part of the direct tide bulge but will remain completely outside the bulge formed by the opposite tide, thus experiencing only a single high tide a day; these are called *diurnal tides*.

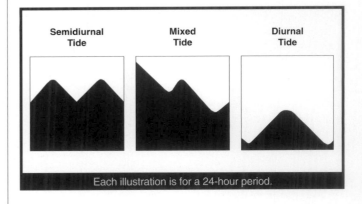

Each illustration is for a 24-hour period.

These statements only apply generally, however, for many different variables can affect tides locally. Researchers have identified as many as 400 such variables, but most are so minor their impacts are very small. Some, however—such as the size and shape of ocean basins, continental land masses, and meteorological tendencies —have major effects. So while it is possible to say, in general, that tides along the Atlantic Coast of North America are semidiurnal in nature, and those along the Pacific Coast are mixed, there are local exceptions.

Other Factors Affecting Tides

The lateral water movements or waves created by the tractive force also are subject to the Coriolis force, named after the French mathematician Gaspard Coriolis, who first described it in 1835. The Coriolis force, a result of the earth's rotation, is perhaps best explained by examining its effect on objects in flight. For example, if you were to fire an artillery shell in a northerly or southerly direction at a distant target (without making the necessary corrections that naval artillerists long ago learned to make), the earth's rotation would cause the target to move out of the path of the shell's flight during the time it took for the shell to complete its journey, and the shot would miss. To an observer watching from the earth's surface, however, it would appear as if the target remained stationary while the artillery shell was deflected; this is because the earth's rotation is not apparent to the observer.

If one considers the earth's atmosphere and oceans as being like the artillery shell, in the sense that they are able to move at least somewhat independently of the earth's solid surface, then it becomes obvious they can be similarly deflected. Wind patterns in the atmosphere, circulation and currents in the oceans, and the movement of ocean waves generated by the tidal force are all deflected by the Coriolis force. In the Northern Hemisphere, tidal flows are deflected in a clockwise direction, or to the right if one is facing north; in the Southern Hemisphere, the effect is in the opposite direction. Along the West Coast of North America this deflection causes tidal waves to propagate northeastward and "lean" against the coastline, resulting in a higher sea level off the coast than in mid-ocean.

Geography and geometry also have much to do with tidal behavior. In part, tidal oscillations are determined by the size and shape of the constraining basin, whether it is a giant ocean basin or a small coastal inlet, bay, or estuary. Variations in ocean depth may alter the direction and speed of the tidal wave, and bottom friction may retard its movement through shallow water.

When the tidal surge strikes the coast itself and moves into its inlets and estuaries, the physical boundaries of these partly enclosed waters may cause resonant oscillations. Nova Scotia's Bay of Fundy is a classic example; there a strong resonant oscillation causes the tidal range to vary from less than 10 feet at the bay's entrance to more than 45 feet at the head of the bay.

Similarly, the shape of the land may cause local differences in sea-level height, as at the opposite ends of a narrow channel, and these differences may produce very strong tidal currents, or delays in the expected times of high or low tide, or both. In estuaries, the tidal crest also travels faster than the tidal trough because the speed of propagation depends upon water depth; thus in estuaries the interval between low and high tides is slightly shorter than the interval between high and low water.

The ragged coastline of the Pacific Northwest, with its countless bays, inlets, islands, channels, and estuaries, offers many opportunities for such local tidal aberrations. The Strait of Juan de Fuca, which separates Washington State's Olympic Peninsula from the southern tip of British Columbia's Vancouver Island, offers an example. After an incoming tidal crest enters the strait, it usually takes two to four hours for it to travel eastward as far as the entrance of Haro Strait, which skirts the eastern shore of

The same estuary at low tide, about 4 1/2 hours later. Now there's not enough water to float a boat, and the bottom is too soft to wade.

Vancouver Island. While the crest is moving in this direction, the shape of the adjacent land masses and the depth of the water in the Strait of Juan de Fuca cause its vertical range to decrease somewhat. Then, when the tidal crest "rounds the corner" of Vancouver Island and enters Haro Strait, some of it is deflected eastward, a result of its own momentum and the Coriolis force, and resulting tides on American shores lying farther eastward will be slightly higher than those along the east coast of Vancouver Island itself. As the tide surges northward into the myriad small bays and ameba-shaped inlets of the Canadian Gulf Islands and the American San Juans, the number of such local aberrations in the tidal range increases a hundred fold.

All these factors, plus many others not mentioned here, create or control the movement of the tides.

Predicting Tides

For as long as men have fished and ships have gone to sea, people have sought to understand tides—no easy task in those distant days when some thought the world was flat and others believed it was the center of the universe, around which all the other planets and the stars revolved.

Most early human societies conceived their own explanations for the observed daily rise and fall of sea water, and these explanations were commonly rooted in animistic or naturalistic religious beliefs. Often tidal movements were attributed to the inhalations and exhalations or other rhythmic movements of great mythic beasts. Typical of these legends was one held by the Maori people of New Zealand, who believed the small tides in Lake Wakatipu were caused by the slow beat of a giant's heart at the bottom of the lake. Other early notions, perhaps a little more firmly grounded in reality, suggested that tides were caused by alternative episodes of evaporation and condensation, or by expansion and contraction of the ocean's water due to changes in its temperature.

But as more and more ancient seafarers patiently measured and recorded the daily differences between the times and heights of tides, it became apparent there was a relationship between the tides and the positions of the sun and moon, even though the exact nature of that relationship was not at first clearly understood.

The earliest written record mentioning an association between the sun, the moon, and the tides comes from writings of the Vedic Period of the Indian subcontinent, dating from 2000 to 1400 B.C., although archeological evidence suggests local inhabitants had a good working knowledge of tides at least several hundred years before that.

Since the Eastern Mediterranean is usually considered the cradle of Western civilization, it may seem surprising that the first observations of astronomical influences on tidal behavior did not come from there. But tidal ranges in the Mediterranean Sea are very small, usually no more than six inches, and Mediterranean seafarers really did not pay much attention to tidal fluctuations until their voyages took them beyond the Mediterranean into other oceans where they encountered large tidal ranges for the first time. The earliest recorded observation of tidal phenomena by an inhabitant of this region was by the Greek historian Herodotus during a visit to the Red Sea around 450 B.C. Aristotle noted tidal action in the Strait of Messina about 325 B.C., and the Greek astronomer Pytheas not only recorded his observations of the tides during a circumnavigation of Britain in 310 B.C., but also remarked on the close relationship between the time of high water and the transit of the moon.

In the course of their trading voyages, Arab seafarers also learned about the nature of tides, leaving scattered written records of their knowledge in various journals, tablets, and treatises dating back at least to 215 B.C., and in legendary sea stories like the *Tales of Sinbad*.

The Chinese also left records of some early understanding of the tides. The rhythmic flow of a tidal bore in the estuary of the Quiantang River was noted as early as 140 B.C. This bore, a tidal wave that periodically swept up the estuary and into the river at flood tide, sometimes caused the water level in the river to rise high enough that a popular crossing could not be used. In about 950 A.D. such an occurrence delayed the crossing of a self-important local king named Qan Miau, who angrily ordered the bore to stop. When it kept coming, he ordered his bowmen to shoot a fusillade of arrows into the advancing wave. Presumably he was even more angry when the arrows failed to stop the advancing tide.

The First Tide Tables

As more and more observers charted tides in relation to the movements of the moon and sun, they could hardly fail to notice a regular pattern, with similar tides occurring whenever the moon and sun reached certain positions in the sky. Since the periodic movements of the moon and sun were well known, it did not require a great leap of logic to figure out they could be used to predict the tides. For example, if an observer noted higher-than-normal tides during each new and full moon, it was then easy enough to predict higher-than-normal tides would occur during the next new- and full-moon periods. This crude system worked well enough for the time, although it obviously did not account for all the observed variations in tides, and nobody understood exactly *why* it worked because the forces involved had not yet been discovered.

Dou Sumong, a late 8th Century Chinese scholar, probably followed this system when he devised a method for calculating the daily difference in the times of tides at various points on the Chinese coast. His predictions were published in tables inscribed on a stone tablet, which disappeared about 180 years later—but not until after another scholar, Wang Xiongfu, had recorded their significance. It is Wang's account that survives today.

Another Chinese observer, Lu Shau, wrote an *Essay on the Tide* in about 850 A.D., in which he referred to early Chinese tide tables that recognized the relationship between spring and neap tides and the phases of the moon; unfortunately, the tables he mentioned have not survived.

Other Chinese tide tables were published early in the 11th Century, and these probably are the oldest surviving tables in the world. All that is known of their origin is that they were prepared sometime before 1056 and were revised in that year by a scholar named Lui Chang Ming. Remarkably, they also were printed in moveable type, some two centuries before publication of Gutenberg's Bible.

As ocean trade expanded, knowledge of the tides spread further around the globe. Arab and Persian navigators who ventured to the coasts of India and China in the 9th Century learned of the twice daily rise and fall of the sea in various harbors and estuaries and noted how these changes caused a reversal in currents. Like their Chinese counterparts, some were quick to recognize the relationship between these changes and the phases of the moon, but others continued to search elsewhere for an explanation. In 902, for example, the Arab scholar Ibn al-Fakih suggested the rise of water he observed in Canton Harbor might be caused by an angel dipping its finger into the China Sea, causing the sea to rise, then drop again when the angel's finger was withdrawn. Perhaps a little uncertain that such a thing could be possible, he also offered an alternative explanation: Maybe, he said, the ebb tide was caused by a giant whale inhaling water, and the high tide came later when the whale finally exhaled.

Another Arab, Al Dimiski of Damascus, had a better handle on things. In 1325 he published remarkably accurate tidal predictions for the mouth of Shatt al Arab, the river formed by the confluence of the Tigris and Euphrates that flows into the northern end of the Persian Gulf. His predictions, intended for use by farmers irrigating their fields near the river's mouth, correctly noted two high and two low tides each day with a lag of slightly less than an hour from the highs and lows of the previous day.

Meanwhile in Western Europe, growing population and increasing trade led to the construction of larger and heavier ships which required more water depth to maneuver and sail; this in turn forced increasing attention on the tides. One early record is an English table, probably prepared by Matthew Paris about 1250, that shows the time of the "Fflod at london brigge." Its usefulness was limited in that it gave only times for high tides in relation to phases of the moon, not for days of the month.

A Spanish atlas published in 1375 was more helpful, containing a diagram showing the times of high and low tides at 14 Western European seaports. Its emphasis on the times of tides, rather than their heights, was typical of early tide tables.

Many Western European ship pilots learned to judge the timing of the tides through years of personal observation and committed the information to memory. One such person, a ship captain skilled in reckoning tides, currents, moons, and harbors, was a character in Chaucer's 1390 *Canterbury Tales*.

An English text published about 1470 included tide

tables that may have been prepared as much as a century earlier. Tables for the Brittany coast of France appeared early in the 16th Century. Records of the same period indicate that in England some individuals made a living predicting tides for certain areas of the coast, keeping to themselves the knowledge of how it was done. In some cases this became a family business, passed along from father to son, and the resulting predictions were published in tables sold to mariners. *The Liverpool Tide Tables*, published by a clergyman named Moses Holden, are an example of this type of publication.

Tidal Theories

These early tide tables and predictions proliferated even though nobody yet completely understood exactly what caused the tides. It remained for Sir Isaac Newton to discover the answer—another Isaac to whom anglers owe a debt. Newton published his *Equilibirum Theory of the Tides* in 1687, describing for the first time the counterbalancing forces of gravity and centrifugal force which keep the earth-moon system in equilibrium and generate the tide-producing forces on earth. Even Newton recognized that his remarkable theory did not explain all the observed variations in the tides, but having discovered the essential forces at work he didn't seem especially interested in pursuing the other factors.

Other mathematicians and scientists did pursue these matters, however, and during the 18th Century several of them, including Bernoulli and Laplace, developed what became known as the dynamic theory of tides. This theory attempted to explain tides in terms of fluids subjected to rhythmic forces. In addition to the equilibrium forces described by Newton, it also considered such factors as the influence of the depth and configuration of ocean basins, inertia, and friction. Over the years it was refined to a point where it could predict tides with considerable accuracy, although it required extremely complex calculations to do so.

Meanwhile, in recognition of their importance, national governments were beginning to take over the business of publishing tide-prediction tables. The British Admiralty published its first set of tables in 1833, followed in 1839 by the French Hydrographic Service, in 1853 by the U.S. Coast and

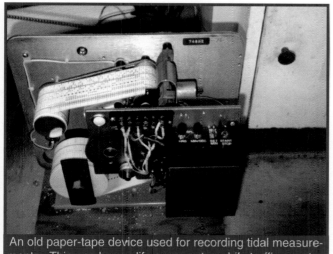
An old paper-tape device used for recording tidal measurements. This one began life as an automobile traffic counter.

Geodetic Survey, and later by other countries. Private publishers also continued to print their own tables, often relying upon the predictions of government agencies.

The first tables published by the U.S. Coast and Geodetic Survey did not contain predictions of daily tides, but this was changed in 1867 when daily predictions were published for 19 main stations and corrections for 124 subordinate stations on both the Atlantic and Pacific Coasts (each coast had its own edition of the tables). Initially the tables gave only the times and heights of high tide, but low tides were added a few years later. In 1896, the tables were expanded to include the entire world, with predictions for 70 main stations and corrections for 3,000 subordinate stations.

Continued refinement of tidal theory in the 19th Century by such scientists as George Airy, Lord Kelvin, and George Darwin in Britain, plus William Ferrel and Rollin A. Harris in the United States, led to development of yet another method of tidal prediction, the harmonic method, which remains in use today. This theory is based on the assumption that actual observed tides are the sum of a number of different components or partial tides, each with a period corresponding to one of the relative astronomical motions of the earth, moon, and sun. Each partial tide also has an amplitude and phase unique to a given location, and these must be measured over long periods to yield a full set of data for all the possible permutations and combinations at each location. Once good data are obtained from observations at a particular location or station, the calculations needed to predict tides at that station are relatively simple and straightforward, although they are very labor-intensive and time-consuming if done by hand.

Tide-Predicting Machines

To ease the onerous task of calculating tide predictions, Lord Kelvin (William Thompson of the University of Glasgow) in 1872 invented a geared machine that could do the calculations mechanically. His machine could sum ten different tidal constituents. A decade later an improved design was developed by William Ferrel of the U.S. Coast and Geodetic Survey, and the best features of both devices were incorporated in yet another machine built in 1912 by R.A. Harris and E.G. Fischer, also of the Coast and Geodetic Survey.

The latter device, at first simply called "Machine No. 2," was a formidable gadget eleven feet long, two feet wide, and six feet high, weighing about 2,500 pounds. It was powered by a hand crank and the results of its calculations were reported on a series of dials. Eventually known to its users as "Old Brass Brains," the machine generated predictions of tidal currents as well as tides, since the principles of both are the same, and it could turn out a year's worth of predictions for a single location in a day's time. It remained in use until 1966, when it was finally replaced by computers.

"Old Brass Brains" could include 37 different variables or components in its calculations, although—as we have seen—this was but a small percentage of the number affecting the tides. The Coast and Geodetic Survey believed that consideration of the 20 to 30 most important variables would result in predictions accurate enough for navigation.

Because the harmonic method of tidal prediction required accurate long-term measurements of tides at many different locations, it also stimulated development of mechanical devices that could precisely measure and record the times and heights of local tides. One such device, introduced about the beginning of the 20th Century, used a weighted float in a "stilling well"—a circular enclosure, or pipe, open at the bottom so water could rise or fall inside, but able to deaden or "still" water-level fluctuations caused by waves. The float was attached to a cable connected to a pen or pencil that was used to draw a continuous track on a roll of paper mounted on a spring-wound drum; as the float rose or fell in response to tidal fluctuations, the track recorded these fluctuations over specified increments of time.

The spring-wound drums in these devices were later replaced with electric motors. Later still, with the advent of early computer systems, some measuring stations were converted from chart rolls to punched paper tape that could be read into computers. Some of the earliest tide-measuring devices also were later replaced with traffic counter-recorders modified for the purpose.

In the United States the agency now responsible for tidal measurement, analysis, and prediction is the National Ocean Survey, a subagency of the National Oceanic and Atmospheric Administration (NOAA). (The name of the National Ocean Survey was changed to the National Ocean Service several years ago, but this prompted so many complaints that the old name was restored.) The National Ocean Survey maintains a network of 168 tidal gaging stations. Most of these are in continental U.S. waters but others are in Hawaii, other Pacific or Indian Ocean islands, and some foreign countries. Although 168 is considered an optimal number of stations, not all are in active service due to funding constraints.

The survey's Pacific Operations Section, based at NOAA's Sand Point campus in Seattle, is responsible for operation and maintenance of all gaging stations on the U.S. West Coast and in the Pacific and Indian Oceans. Its nine-member staff services tide gages scattered from Prudhoe Bay, Alaska, to the tip of South America, and as far west as Diego Garcia in the Indian Ocean. Its counterpart, the Atlantic Operations Section, based in Chesapeake, Virginia, is responsible for gaging stations on the Great Lakes, the East Coast, the Gulf of Mexico, and the Atlantic Ocean.

Within the past five years the National Ocean Survey has replaced its older tide-measuring devices with what is called the Next Generation Water Level Measuring System (NGWLMS). The new electronic gages that make up the system continue to rely upon stilling wells, but they no longer use weighted floats; instead, each stilling well is fitted at the top with a device that generates an acoustic (sound) signal once a second, then measures the time it takes for an echo to return from the surface of the water inside the stilling well. With this information it can calculate the exact height of the water, or tide, inside the stilling well. These acoustic generators aren't much to look at, but if you stand next to one you can easily hear its regular, once-a-second, electronic "click."

Each of these gages generates a continuous flow of digital information that feeds an electronic storage device, which in turn automatically transmits the data every three hours via satellite to a central data-collection station at Wallops Island, Maryland. From there it goes into the National Ocean Survey's central computer data base at Silver Spring, Maryland. This data base resides on comput-

A modern acoustic tide gage. A device in the knob-like structure at the top fires an acoustic signal down the tube to the water, then measures the time it takes for the echo to return.

ers built by the Digital Equipment Company, the same machines used to compute tide and tidal-current predictions.

Some of the old analog tide gages with their weighted floats and revolving drums or paper-tape machines have been left in place next to their new acoustic counterparts for purposes of comparison. Data from both the old and new machines will be collected for several years and compared to assure the accuracy of the new system. Greater accuracy is only one of the perceived advantages of the new acoustic devices; automation is another—with automatic data storage and satellite transmission, it will no longer be necessary for a person to record information manually off paper charts or process rolls of paper tape.

Using measurements from the network of gaging stations and custom software written for the purpose, the National Ocean Survey's computers generate tidal predictions. The agency's software considers about 115 different components or variables in making the calculations; again, more could be considered, but the resulting increase in accuracy would be so slight it is not believed worth the extra effort to include additional factors in the software.

Until 1995, NOAA published its tidal predictions for sale to the public. Then Congress, in its infinite wisdom, decided that this function should be "privatized," and beginning in 1996 NOAA ceased publishing tide tables. Instead, it now furnishes raw data to private publishers so they can use it to prepare their own tables for sale to the public.

Understanding Tide Tables

To be useful, tide-prediction tables must have some sort of standard baseline or common reference point from which to measure. In nautical nomenclature, this reference point is called the *datum line*, and for purposes of tidal measurement it is considered zero. A positive value (or plus symbol) in a tide table means the water level will be higher than the datum line; a negative value (or minus symbol) means the tide will fall below that line. One of the main reasons for recording tidal measurements over a long period is to obtain enough information to establish the datum line accurately.

The datum line also serves another important purpose: It is the reference level for the depths shown on charts used for navigation. By international agreement, datum is selected at a point low enough that few tides, if any, will fall below it—but the agreement stops short of defining exactly where that point should be. At some time in the past, the U.S. Coast and Geodetic Survey established East Coast datum as the mean low-water line—the average height of low waters measured over an 18.6-year period during which most possible astronomical permutations affecting tides will occur. But on the West Coast, datum was established as mean lower low water—the average height of the lower of two tides each day over the same span of 18.6 years. These decisions were not made arbitrarily; they reflect the different types of tides that commonly occur on each coast—semidiurnal tides (similar in height and spaced equally apart in time) on the Atlantic Coast, mixed tides (twice daily tides of unequal height) on the Pacific.

This discrepancy was finally corrected in 1989 when the datum line was changed to mean lower low water for all U.S. stations. The practical effect was to change the way tides are measured on the Atlantic Coast, and although in most cases the difference is very slight—a couple of tenths of a foot or less—charts published after 1989 should be used for maximum accuracy.

To make matters a little more confusing, Canada uses another datum. On the West Coast, datum in Canadian waters is defined as the water level at the "lowest normal tides"—a point slightly lower than the average measured low tides used by the U.S. National Ocean Survey to compute mean lower low water. This means the U.S. datum is slightly higher than the Canadian datum, and U.S. tide tables therefore show negative values more often than Canadian tables. Again, the differences are small enough to be of only minor importance, especially to anglers fishing from small, shallow-draft boats. But anglers and mariners alike should always be careful to use U.S. tide tables with U.S. charts and Canadian tide tables with Canadian charts, and not use tide tables from one country with charts from the other, or vice versa.

If tide tables and charts from the same country are used together, then the actual water depth can always be established by adding the height of the predicted tide at a given time to the datum shown on a nautical chart for a given location; that is, the chart datum plus the value of the predicted tide equals the actual water depth.

It should be noted that datum does not mean the same thing as sea level. Datum is determined by measuring the average of the lowest tides while mean sea level is computed by averaging *all* tides, including high waters. Because low tides vary by location along coastlines, the datum level also changes from place to place.

In the United States, the National Ocean Survey computes predicted tides for the Central and Western Pacific and Indian Oceans, the East Coast of North and South America including Greenland, Europe and the West Coast of Africa including the Mediterranean Sea, the West Coast of North and South America including the Hawaiian Islands, and Alaska. The West Coast tables include predictions for 40 main stations and about 1,220 subordinate stations in North and South America. All these tables were published in book form until 1996.

In Canada, the Department of Fisheries and Oceans publishes predicted tide and current tables for the Atlantic Coast and Bay of Fundy, the Gulf of St. Lawrence, the St. Lawrence and Saguenay Rivers, the Arctic and Hudson Bay, Juan de Fuca Strait and the Strait of Georgia, and Barkley Sound and Discovery Passage to Dixon Entrance.

Rather than rely upon government publications, most anglers and boaters traditionally have gotten their tide information from commercially published tide-table booklets. This was true even before Congress directed NOAA to stop publishing tide tables. The commercially published booklets, widely sold at sporting-goods stores and marinas, usually contain predicted times and heights of daily high and low tides for specific local areas—a few main gaging or reference stations, plus correction tables for a limited number of subordinate stations.

The predictions for main reference stations are typically expressed in numerical values, positive for tides above the datum line, negative for tides expected to fall below the line. The correction tables are based on a comparison of the times and water heights at the main reference station and a subordinate station; again, the differences are expressed numerically in positive and negative values. For example, if the predicted high tide at a main reference station is 10 feet at 11 a.m local time, and the correction table for a nearby subordinate station reads +0.5 feet, -10 minutes, it means high tide at the subordinate station is expected to be a half-foot higher and occur 10 minutes earlier than at the main reference station.

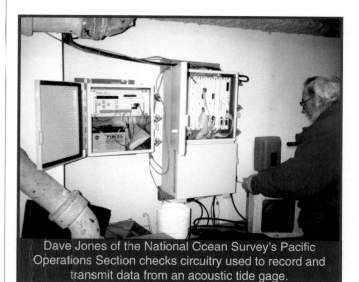

Dave Jones of the National Ocean Survey's Pacific Operations Section checks circuitry used to record and transmit data from an acoustic tide gage.

Sooke Harbor, British Columbia
November 1994

Day		Time		Ht./Ft.	
1		0520		5.3	
Tue		1125		9.1	
		1845		2.9	
2		0055		7.4	
Wed		0605		5.7	
		1150		9.6	
		1935		2.0	
3		0155		7.6	
Thu		0640		6.1	
		1220		10.0	
		2020		1.3	

Excerpt from a typical numeric tide table.

Most tide-prediction and correction tables show only the times and heights of high or low water—that is, the extremes of the tides. They do not show what the tide will be doing between those extremes, and in that respect they are of somewhat limited usefulness, especially to anglers. Far more useful are graphic tide tables that show the approximate stage of the tide at any moment. These tables display a plotted line showing the tidal curve for each day, which makes it possible to tell at a glance the height of the tide as well as its approximate angle of advance or retreat—just the kind of information a fisherman most needs to know. These tables are not absolutely precise because of the method used to calculate the tidal curves, but they are certainly accurate enough for an angler's purposes. Graphic tide tables are published commercially in calendar form, and with one of these calendars it is easy to trace the cycle of the tides for any day, week, or month, or for an entire year.

The only problem with these calendars is that they are published for only a few main reference stations, and if an angler plans to fish somewhere else—as most anglers do,

since main reference stations are often in busy, urban harbors—then he is again faced with the problem of applying corrections for a subordinate station. This is bothersome enough when dealing with a conventional tide table, but it becomes a real challenge when the correction must be applied to a graphically plotted tidal curve. Fortunately, in most cases the corrections probably are not significant enough to worry about, and if they are, then there is a manual method that can be used to plot a "customized" tidal curve. This is done by using the times and values for the nearest main reference station, applying corrections for the subordinate station nearest the area for which the tidal curve is being plotted, then using what is called the *one-quarter, one-tenth rule* to plot the actual curve on a sheet of graph paper. This is the same method commercial publishers use to plot tidal curves, and while it is not complex, it is labor-intensive and does take time. A complete explanation of the method is included in any of the National Ocean Survey tide tables published before 1996,

Happily, better solutions are now available in the form of personal computer programs. Probably the most sophisticated of these is *Tides and Currents for Windows*, by Nautical Software, 14657 S.W. Teal Blvd., Beaverton, Oregon 97007. This program can rapidly calculate and plot predicted tides at both main and subordinate reference stations and print the results in any of several different graphic formats. It allows users to generate graphic tide tables for any of the National Ocean Survey's 40 main reference stations and 1,220 subordinate stations on the Pacific Coast, or even create customized graphic tables for subordinate stations not listed by the survey. The program also is capable of producing tables showing the height of tide at any main or subordinate station at one-minute intervals for any given day. It provides the latitude and longitude of each main or subordinate station, the local time of sunrise and sunset, and any notes to mariners that may apply to a particular station. It even adjusts automatically for daylight savings time! An Atlantic Coast version also is available.

Another program, *Tides*, is available for personal computers using the Microsoft or IBM DOS operating systems. This program, written by Edward P. Wallner, 32 Barney Hill Road, Wayland, Massachusetts 01778-3602, is considered "shareware" and is available to users for a $15 registration fee; it

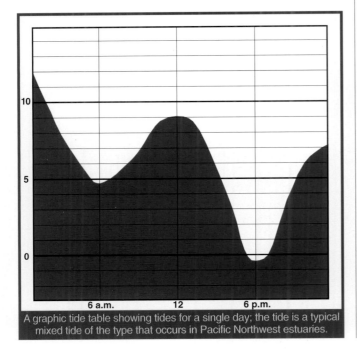

A graphic tide table showing tides for a single day; the tide is a typical mixed tide of the type that occurs in Pacific Northwest estuaries.

10

5

0

6 a.m.   12   6 p.m.

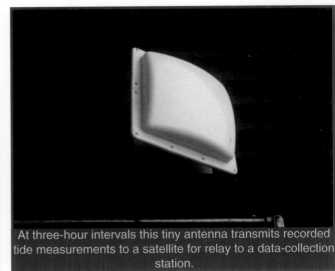

At three-hour intervals this tiny antenna transmits recorded tide measurements to a satellite for relay to a data-collection station.

also can be downloaded from the Internet. A menu-driven program, it computes tides and currents and displays the output on a monitor or sends it to a printer. It comes with data for main reference stations used by the National Ocean Survey, plus selected foreign stations. Additional primary stations can be added by entering the appropriate constituents and subordinate stations can be added simply by entering correction data. *Tides* lacks some of the sophisticated features of *Tides and Currents for Windows*, but it does the basic task well. Other tide-prediction programs also are available, including some written specifically for local areas.

The ease, convenience, and versatility of these programs may well render conventional published tide tables and graphic tide calendars obsolete. But there will always be a need for somebody to maintain tide gages, record their measurements, and calculate predicted tides and currents, so there should always be plenty of work for the National Ocean Survey, the Canadian Department of Fisheries and Oceans, and their counterparts in other nations.

Even with the best information and the most accurate predictions, anglers may still encounter situations when the tide springs a surprise. Estuary anglers, who fish the countless small nooks and crannies of the coastline—places where tide records have never been kept—are especially likely to find the tides behaving in unexpected ways.

Estuaries with small openings to the sea are among the most likely places to show tidal aberrations. One estuary I fish often is located less than 10 miles from the nearest subordinate tide station, but its tides lag as much as two hours behind. The reason is that the estuary has a narrow entrance partly blocked by a sand bar that restricts the flow of water in and out, so when the tide reaches maximum ebb at the subordinate station, water is still draining out of the estuary; conversely, the incoming tide must reach a certain height before water can spill over the sand bar and begin filling the estuary, so it does not begin to feel the first effects of a rising tide until well after the tide has begun running beyond the bar.

I found this out the hard way, relying on published predictions for the nearby subordinate station when I first fished the estuary. I launched my boat on an outgoing tide, confident the flood tide would come at the predicted time and provide enough water for me to return to my launching point well before dark. But darkness came and the flood tide did not, and I spent several hours sitting in my boat stranded on a sandbar until the flood tide finally did come, long after night had fallen. Wives find such excuses difficult to accept.

From that experience and others, I now have an idea of what to expect when fishing this estuary and I can plan accordingly. Sometimes there is simply no substitute for such hard-earned experience or local knowledge.

Which brings up another point: Most anglers and boaters accept tide-table predictions as if they were Holy Writ, as certain as the date or the time of local sunrise or sunset. It's important to remember they are *only predictions*, and even though they are many times more accurate and dependable than weather forecasts, there are still occasions when actual tides will vary from those predicted. As the National Ocean Survey warns: "Each water-level station is unique; there is no single standard of accuracy when comparing astronomic tide predictions with observed water levels." In other words, mariners beware.

When it was still in the business of publishing its own

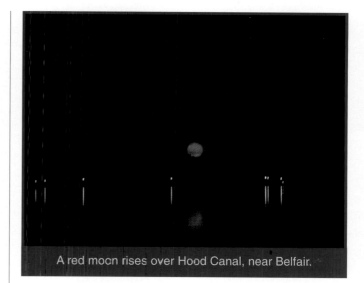

A red moon rises over Hood Canal, near Belfair.

tables of predicted tides, the National Ocean Survey routinely included a chart showing the standard and average differences between predicted and actual times and heights of tides at main reference stations. The differences were almost always small, but there were almost always differences—illustrating the point that tide predictions are not always accurate. This is not surprising, considering that local tides may be affected by as many as 400 different variables.

Meteorological factors probably have the greatest influence on differences between predicted and actual tides. NOAA studies have shown that a drop in barometric pressure equivalent to one inch of mercury may cause the local sea level to rise as much as a foot, which would mean high tides at least a foot higher than predicted. Since extreme low-pressure areas are often accompanied by strong winds, the simultaneous occurrence of both also may lead to a "storm tide"—a normally high tide made even higher by the combined effects of low atmospheric pressure and strong winds. This combination of circumstances also frequently results in a hurricane, and since most anglers have the good sense to stay away from the water when a hurricane is pending, they aren't likely to encounter such extremes.

Nevertheless, anglers may occasionally witness tidal changes caused by less extreme weather conditions. Strong, continuing onshore winds can cause waters to "pile up," increasing the height of predicted local tides. Offshore winds may have the opposite effect. A strong, stable, high-pressure system that remains over one area of the ocean for an extended period also can cause water to flow toward other areas where the atmospheric pressure is lower, so tides will be slightly lower than predicted in the vicinity of the high-pressure system and slightly higher in areas of lower pressure.

These situations usually cause only small differences between actual and predicted tides, but the point is worth restating: Numeric tide tables and the plotted lines on graphic tide calendars are only predictions, and while science and mathematics have gone to great lengths to assure their accuracy, the vagaries of weather or local conditions can occasionally lead to surprises.

There remains one other great question about the tide: Which tide is best to fish? An answer will be found in the next chapter.

VII
OBSERVATIONS OF FISH
AND TIDES

When I began fishing estuaries more than a quarter of a century ago, conventional wisdom—if "wisdom" truly is what it was—held that the best time to go fishing was on a rising tide. That observation was applied mainly to sea-run cutthroat, since then, as now, they provided the closest thing to a year-round estuary fishery in the Seattle area, where I live.

In retrospect, it is hardly surprising that a rising tide was preferred. Anglers seeking sea-run cutthroat nearly always find themselves fishing in shallow water, often close to the beach in the thinnest margins of the tide, so a rising tide usually holds more promise of favorable fishing conditions. Most probably it was simply this need to have enough water for fishing that gave rise to the notion that high tides were always best; after all, if water is lacking, fish surely will be lacking too.

The rising-tide approach was pretty much an article of faith in those days, but even then a few anglers were beginning to question whether it might also be profitable to fish other tides. That question led inevitably to others: Where did fish, particularly sea-run cutthroat, go when the tide went out? Where did they stay during low tides? Did their behavior change on different stages of the tide? Did they react differently during slack-water periods than during times of strong water movement? All these were very good questions, and the more they were asked the more estuary anglers began to realize how little they actually knew about the habits and behavior of sea-run cutthroat and other estuarine fish.

Some looked for answers in the pages of the scientific literature, but found few of them; even less was known about sea-run cutthroat then than is the case now, and what little scientific work had been done up to that time did not address the questions anglers were asking. That left only the inconsistent, unsystematic, and often unreliable personal observations of anglers themselves to go on, and that was not much.

Eventually all this conjecture and speculation reached critical mass among members of the Washington Fly Fishing Club, who decided to launch their own investigation into sea-run cutthroat behavior, especially to find out where sea-runs went when the tide was out. To accomplish this they decided to use sonic tags, which only recently had been developed by the National Marine Fisheries Service to track the movements of salmon and steelhead in the Columbia River. The NMFS had come up with a miniature battery-operated sound transmitter housed in a plastic capsule small enough to fit in the stomach of a fish. When the transmitter was activated and the fish was released, its movements could be followed with directional hydrophones capable of picking up the high-frequency sound pulses emitted by the transmitter.

More than 30 club members signed up to participate in the cutthroat experiment, donating money to buy several sonic tags and borrowing tracking gear from the government. Dewatto Bay, a sheltered, mile-long estuary where the little Dewatto River drains into Hood Canal, was chosen as the site for the experiment, scheduled for a long weekend in October 1971.

Beach seines were employed in an effort to capture some cutthroat for use in the experiment. The seines turned up plenty of sea perch, flounder, and herring, but not a single cutthroat—perhaps further evidence, if any were needed, that anglers didn't know much about the habits of these fish. This dilemma was finally solved by Ed Foss, a veteran sea-run cutthroat angler, who hooked and landed a 15-inch cutthroat on a fly; this fish quickly became the first subject of the experiment. It was anesthetized, a transmitter capsule was worked down its gullet into its stomach, and when it had recovered from the anesthesia it was released so tracking could begin. Meanwhile, continued beach seining finally netted a second cutthroat, and this fish, about 19 inches long, received a second transmitter.

Club members tracked both fish around the clock for the next several days. Listening through hydrophones, they

Near the end of the fight. This sea-run cutthroat was hooked on a dry fly in a Puget Sound estuary.

Releasing a sea-run hooked in one of numerous small estuaries along Hood Canal, Washington.

took directional bearings on sound pulses emitted by the transmitter in each fish, then moved the tracking boat to another location where a second bearing was taken. The position of the fish was then plotted by triangulation and noted on a chart, along with the time and date of the observation. By this method a continuous track was made of the movements of each fish.

When the experiment was over and the results were analyzed, they revealed both fish had spent most of their time in the shallow waters inside Dewatto Bay. Each displayed a tendency to head farther into the estuary on a rising tide and farther out on an outgoing tide, especially when water depth fell to only three feet above datum. When they chose to remain in the inner estuary during low tide, both fish usually moved into the river channel where the water was deeper. When they left the estuary on an outgoing tide, they tended to return on the next flood tide, again when the water level rose to about three feet above datum. Each fish also made one unexplained "side trip," one directly out into the deep, open water of Hood Canal, then back to the estuary, the other to a small cove about two miles down the beach from Dewatto Bay, where it lingered only about 20 minutes before starting back again.

These results indicated some tendencies toward patterned behavior, but no definitive evidence of consistent responses at different stages of the tide. About the only real conclusion that could be drawn from the experiment was that it probably was a good idea to fish the shallows carefully and always to fish tides above three feet. But veteran estuary anglers already knew these things.

After participating in the experiment and spending several hours in the middle of a cold, foggy night listening to eerie pulses of sound coming from the belly of a fish, I shared in the collective frustration over the lack of more definitive results. Thinking about it afterward, though, I decided our expectations probably had been too high; we had thought we would find a clear pattern of behavior and the answers to all our questions—in effect, the Holy Grail of sea-run cutthroat fishing. Maybe there *was* no pattern; perhaps the movements of sea-run cutthroat trout, and other fish, are simply random.

The more I thought about it, however, the more diffi-

culty I had accepting that idea. The need to find logical or consistent patterns in nature seems deeply ingrained in the human psyche, an inescapable part of our character. We organize our own lives in patterns, establishing daily routines that we follow almost without conscious thought, and we expect to find similar patterns elsewhere, including the behavior of our fellow creatures—though we often forget they live their lives by different sets of rules.

Yet the behavior of all of earth's creatures, human and otherwise, is in some measure driven by the daily cycles of sunlight and darkness and the seasonal cycles of warm weather and cold; these influence or control such basic biological functions as the timing of sleep, migration, feeding, and reproduction. Tides are yet another natural cycle, and in the estuaries they clearly influence or control the biological activities of many animals, especially those incapable of rapid movement. Are fish exempt from the influence of the tides simply because they are able to move around easily? Or are their movements also driven, at least in part, by the daily rise and fall of water? Intuitively, it seemed to me the answer must be that even rapidly moving creatures like the sea-run cutthroat were subject to influence by the tides, and that any search for patterns in their behavior should be correlated with the daily rise and fall of water.

The Washington Fly Fishing Club's sonic-tracking experiment essentially had been an attempt to test that theory, but in retrospect it seemed to me that observations of only two fish over a single long weekend were not enough to yield definitive results. Yet tracking a pair of cutthroat for even that brief time had suggested at least the possibility of consistent behavior in response to tidal movements, and I took that as a sign of encouragement that helped me to decide to continue searching on my own.

But just how to go about this was something of a problem. If 30 members of the Washington Fly Fishing Club using sophisticated equipment had failed in the attempt, what could a single angler, without such equipment, possibly do that might yield better results? After much thought, I decided the answer was to observe and record the behavior of fish systematically over a long period of time, then search for the existence of patterns if any were there to be found.

Yet how would I make such observations? Sea-run cutthroat are certainly among the most visible of estuarine fish, often revealing their presence by rising or jumping, but even sea-runs don't do this predictably; there are undoubtedly more occasions when they choose to remain invisible than otherwise, and an observer can hardly record the presence of fish he cannot see. Something much more dependable than the cutthroat's occasional willingness to jump or rise of its own accord was needed to carry out a meaningful long-term program of observation.

This was a dilemma I pondered for several years until the answer finally came unexpectedly with a change in angling tactics. Like most sea-run cutthroat anglers, I had always used sinking lines and wet flies in the estuaries, even when I found cutthroat rising ("conventional wisdom" again). Then one day it suddenly occurred to me that this approach made no sense at all. In fresh water, the way to catch a rising trout is to use a floating fly; why should trout in salt water be any different? Even if there was nothing apparent on the surface that would cause sea-runs to rise—which usually was the case—wouldn't it still make more sense to fish to rising cutthroat with a floating fly?

These thoughts led me to begin experimenting with floating lines and dry flies in the estuaries, and suddenly a whole new world opened up. I discovered that sea-run cutthroat would come to a dry fly far more eagerly and consistently than they had ever come to any wet flies I had ever used. Not only that, but I also found there were many more sea-runs in the estuaries than I had ever suspected. Where before I could usually count on seeing only a few fish rise during a day's fishing, I now found that with a dry fly I could stimulate them to rise almost at will. Even when I cast over water that gave no hint or sign of fish, the dry fly often brought up cutthroat whose existence otherwise would have remained hidden—and many more of them than I had ever dreamed there were. They came nipping or rolling to the fly, often several at a time, sometimes taking it and sometimes not, but in each case disclosing their presence. Here, I realized, was not just a marvelous and exciting new way to fish, but also the solution to my problem: The dry fly seemed to offer a reliable means of locating cutthroat that otherwise would have gone undetected. At last I could proceed with the experiment I had long had in mind.

The concept of the experiment was simple, as it necessarily had to be for a one-man, non-scientific effort: I would systematically record every confirmed sighting of a sea-run cutthroat and plot the results in half-hour increments on a graph superimposed over a chart of the day's tidal movements. My hope was that over time this would reveal any patterns that might exist in the way sea-run cutthroat respond to tidal changes.

I decided that a "confirmed sighting" would include a cutthroat actually caught, or one hooked and lost, or one seen jumping, or one seen rising, either in response to my fly or of its own accord. This seemed to fit the purpose of the experiment, which was simply to establish the active presence of sea-runs and determine any correlation between their movements and the tides. Of course I understood this definition also allowed the possibility of error—other fish besides cutthroat do rise occasionally, especially coho, which often share the same water, and I might unwittingly count them as cutthroat. But years of estuary fishing experience had taught me that even when cutthroat and coho are intermingled in the same waters, 85 to 90 percent of the rising fish will be cutthroat. Steelhead and other species of Pacific salmon also rise in salt water, but they are usually present in the estuaries only for a short period during their seasonal migrations, and most of the time a careful observer can distinguish their rise forms from those of cutthroat. For all these reasons, I felt confident that counting rises, along with other sightings, would be a legitimate way to measure the presence of sea-run cutthroat, even though some erroneous sightings might enter in. In any case, I vowed to be as conservative as possible in evaluating each sighting, disregarding any surface disturbance that I did not feel certain had been caused by a fish.

I also understood there were many other variables that could affect my observations. I knew I would be fishing in different locations and in different seasons. I knew the weather would always be changing, along with the air temperature and the intensity and duration of light. Wind probably would make observations completely impossible on some days and difficult on others. The presence of predators, such as seals, sea lions, otters, or even other human anglers, might well disrupt any normal patterns of fish behavior. All these and countless other factors would pose an infinite number of changing circumstances that could never be measured accurately or taken fully into account. That being so, I decided simply to ignore all of them, reasoning that if I continued observations over a long enough time all these other factors would eventually balance out and I would be left with a record of the only two things I really wanted to measure—numbers of cutthroat seen, and the stage of tide when they were observed.

There was, however, one other limitation I knew I could not overcome—or, more properly, which I chose not to try to overcome. I am addicted to the pursuit of freshwater trout and steelhead during May, June, July, and August, and I was unwilling to abandon those pursuits even in favor of trying to solve the mysteries of cutthroat behavior. It's not that I neglect the estuaries altogether during summer, but I knew I probably would not be fishing them often enough to gather sufficient data for valid results. So I decided to limit my observations to the eight-month period from September through April, when I do most of my estuary fishing.

I also decided to limit the hours during which I would observe and record fish activity from 9:30 a.m. to 4 p.m. each day. There were some practical reasons for this, including the important one that it is seldom light before 8 a.m. or much after 4 p.m. during winter months at this latitude, and usually I spend the first part of each day getting wherever it is I plan to fish. It's true that fall and spring months provide more daylight, and during those times I often start fishing earlier than 9:30 a.m. and quit later than 4 p.m., but my purpose was to gather data for comparison, and in order for comparisons to be valid the data had to be collected over the same period each day. Hence 9:30 a.m. to 4 p.m.

Having made these ground rules, I began observations during the first week of January 1976. Mentally I had made a long-term commitment to the experiment, but had not really bothered to define what "long-term" might mean; in the event, it turned out to be much longer than I ever expected. I continued making observations until late January, 1994, a period of slightly more than 18 years, finally calling a halt only to begin analyzing the data for this book. By coincidence, that 18-year span is nearly equivalent to the period during which all common astronomical permutations affecting tides will occur, and during those 18 years I fished every range of tide, from extreme lows to extreme highs.

Many hundreds of hours of observations were made at three different locations on Puget Sound and two on Hood Canal, with each half-hour's worth of fish sightings (or lack thereof) carefully recorded. It took more than a little time and effort to write down the results, total them up at day's end, then plot them in graphic form, and I soon fell into the habit of setting aside each day's observations without making any ongoing effort to evaluate or compare them

The Union River estuary, Washington, on a late autumn day.

with previous observations. After a while I realized I was accumulating a vast amount of raw data that would take a major effort to collate, sort, and analyze, and the longer I waited to do that the more work it was going to be. Despite that realization, other demands kept me from the task, and even while I delayed tackling the mound of unsorted reports, I continued adding to them, recording more observations each time I went fishing. The stack of daily charts grew ever higher.

At length I realized I had gathered so much information I did not even know *how* I would organize or analyze all of it. Personal computers provided the answer; they hadn't existed when I started the experiment, but fortunately they came along in time to offer a solution. But even with the help of a computer, I could see it would take considerable work to set up a series of spreadsheets to analyze all the information I had gathered, then enter and format the data and actually do the analysis, and I began to think this job would have to await my retirement when I might finally have time to do it. As it turned out, that's exactly what happened.

When I finally did get down to work, it took a couple of weeks to set up the methods and programs needed to analyze the data, plus another full week to enter and format the raw numbers. Part of that time also was spent entering tide-table data and local-station corrections for years before 1980, all of which had to be calculated by hand—a simple but time-consuming task. For later years, the work was greatly simplified by using the *Tides and Currents for Windows* software described in the previous chapter, which automatically calculated local-station corrections and tidal heights for each half-hour period.

At last everything was ready and I started the computer on the job of actually collating and sorting the data. The answers I had sought for so many years, if they existed at all, lay buried somewhere in all those raw numbers, and I felt a rising sense of anticipation as the computer sorted the information and finally began printing the results. The reports spilled out one after another in a series of print-outs that ultimately measured nearly a hundred feet in length, and the numbers on the bottom lines of these reports were transferred to a series of computer-generated graphs and charts to display the results in visual form.

Based on impressions I had gained from many years of fishing for sea-run cutthroat, I thought I had a pretty good idea what the results would show, so it was very much of a surprise when they revealed that a great deal of what I had thought I knew about sea-run cutthroat behavior probably wasn't true at all. The figures showed conclusively that the times of day, tides, and amounts of water movement I had thought best for fishing were not necessarily optimal after all. In most cases the differences weren't striking, but my own statistics had proven many of my earlier impressions were wrong.

The findings also showed evidence of patterns in the way sea-run cutthroat respond to tidal changes, as I had always suspected, but it took some digging to find out where and what the patterns were—and when they finally emerged, they were not quite what I had expected they would be, nor were they always as clear-cut as I had hoped they might be.

The overall results, based on totals from all observations over the 18-year period of the experiment, were plotted on a graph showing the average height of tide for each half-hour of observation and the average number of fish sighted during each half-hour period:

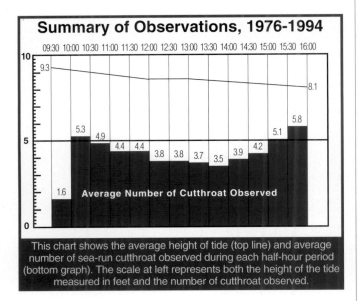

Summary of Observations, 1976-1994

This chart shows the average height of tide (top line) and average number of sea-run cutthroat observed during each half-hour period (bottom graph). The scale at left represents both the height of the tide measured in feet and the number of cutthroat observed.

The average height of the tide is shown as a line across the top of the graph. This nearly straight line is the result you would expect from averaging the values of hundreds of different tides, with highs and lows occurring almost any time of day. But the line does have a slight downward trend, from 9.3 to 8.1 feet, indicating that over the 18-year period of the experiment I probably fished more ebb tides than floods, which was something of a surprise.

The figures also reveal a marked bias for high tides; the daily mean high water for all the days on which observations were made was 8.57 feet, compared with a daily mean of 7.2 feet for the five sites where the observations were made. That meant the tides I fished averaged nearly 1.4 feet higher than the average of all tides at the five locations. This wasn't a surprise because I had purposely chosen tides I knew would provide enough water to launch and recover a small boat at the locations I was fishing, and such tides tend to be higher than average. Whether this bias had any bearing or effect on the results of the observations is impossible to say.

The average number of fish observed during each half-hour increment over the 18 years varied from a low of 1.6 during the period from 9:30 to 10 a.m. to a high of 5.8 during the half hour from 3:30 to 4 p.m. (variations in the number of sightings per half hour appear somewhat exaggerated by the scale on the graph). The relatively small

number of fish sighted during the first half hour of each day (9:30 to 10 a.m.) remains unexplained; I can only speculate it might have been due to the fact that I was not always in the best position to observe cutthroat during the first half hour of fishing, since it often took a little time to reach the places experience had taught me were most likely to hold cutthroat. Another possibility is that the fish may not have been very active during the low temperatures of cold winter mornings.

Converting the figures from this chart to hourly (rather than half-hour) increments yielded an overall average of 8.4 cutthroat sightings per hour; in other words, during the 18 years I kept records of cutthroat activity, I observed (saw, hooked, or caught) an average of 8.4 fish every hour. Afternoons, with 8.45 fish per hour, were slightly better than mornings, with 8.20, but the difference was too small to be statistically significant. The only surprise here was that the numbers were so high; remembering what seemed like more than a few blank fishing days during those 18 years, I had not expected figures like these.

The graph also indicates the periods from 10 to 11 a.m. and 3 to 4 p.m. were most productive, but this is without any adjustments to account for incoming or outgoing tides, stage of tide, water height or movement, etc., so it would be premature to draw any conclusions from this graph about whether those hours are the best to fish.

A second graph was prepared to compare sighting observations made during incoming and outgoing tides:

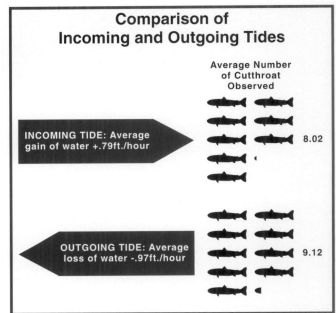

Comparison of Incoming and Outgoing Tides

Average Number of Cutthroat Observed

INCOMING TIDE: Average gain of water +.79ft./hour — 8.02

OUTGOING TIDE: Average loss of water -.97ft./hour — 9.12

This comparison shows that a few more fish were seen during outgoing tides, but again the difference was small enough to be considered insignificant.

One impression I had formed as a result of my angling experience was that sea-run cutthroat were most active and visible during the two hours before or after a change of either high or low tide, so I decided to test whether that was in fact the case. Observation data for the two-hour periods on either side of a change of tide was extracted and plotted graphically, with the following results:

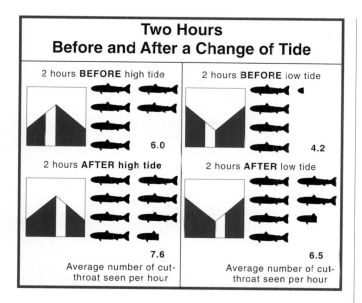

Two Hours
Before and After a Change of Tide

2 hours BEFORE high tide

6.0

2 hours BEFORE low tide

4.2

2 hours AFTER high tide

7.6

2 hours AFTER low tide

6.5

Average number of cutthroat seen per hour

Average number of cutthroat seen per hour

Much to my surprise, this report showed fewer fish were seen during these periods than during the rest of the tide cycle. During the last two hours of a high tide, an average of only 6.0 fish per hour were seen, while during the first two hours after the tide had turned the average was 7.6 per hour; both figures were less than the average of 8.02 per hour during all incoming tides. The low-tide figures showed even more of a discrepancy.

The obvious conclusion was that other times must be more productive than the two hours on either side of a change of tide. Since I had already considered the first and last two hours of every tide cycle, that left only the middle, so I extracted the observation data from only the middle two hours of each tide cycle and plotted the results. These confirmed that the middle portion of the tide was indeed most productive, with some very interesting figures:

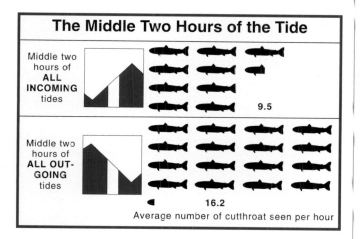

The Middle Two Hours of the Tide

Middle two hours of **ALL INCOMING** tides

9.5

Middle two hours of **ALL OUT-GOING** tides

16.2

Average number of cutthroat seen per hour

While these numbers are not adjusted for morning vs. afternoon tides, water height, or water movement, they appear to show that more fish are present and active during the middle two hours of each tide cycle, especially during an outgoing tide. In fact, the average number of fish observed during the middle hours of an outgoing tide was nearly twice that seen during the middle hours of an incoming tide. This was the first major surprise from the data, effectively laying to rest my impression that the two hours before or after a change of tide were the best times

to fish. It also pretty much destroyed the old myth that an incoming tide is best to fish.

Of course these figures do not mean an angler should *always* expect to see 16 fish an hour during the middle of an outgoing tide. The data that led to this result included many periods of observation when few, if any, fish were seen; conversely, they included many periods when more than 16 fish were sighted or hooked. What these numbers really suggest is there is a greater potential for encountering fish during the middle portion of the tide than at other times.

Does it matter if the tide is in the morning or the afternoon? Another graph was set up to try to answer that question:

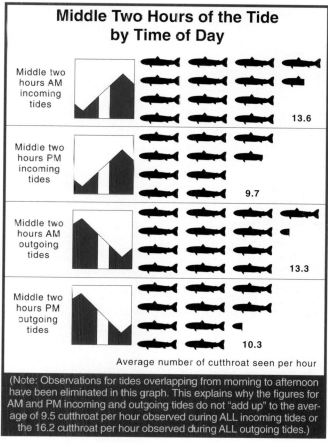

Middle Two Hours of the Tide
by Time of Day

Middle two hours AM incoming tides

13.6

Middle two hours PM incoming tides

9.7

Middle two hours AM outgoing tides

13.3

Middle two hours PM outgoing tides

10.3

Average number of cutthroat seen per hour

(Note: Observations for tides overlapping from morning to afternoon have been eliminated in this graph. This explains why the figures for AM and PM incoming and outgoing tides do not "add up" to the average of 9.5 cutthroat per hour observed during ALL incoming tides or the 16.2 cutthroat per hour observed during ALL outgoing tides.)

Morning-to-afternoon overlapping tides have been eliminated from this graph, with the result that the average number of sightings per hour during both morning (13.3) and afternoon (10.3) outgoing tides is less than the average for all outgoing tides (16.2). This suggests the best outgoing tide may actually be one that overlaps from morning to afternoon. For incoming tides, morning appears best.

The next question was whether there was any correlation between speed of water movement and presence of fish. To calculate the answer it was necessary to divide the speed of water movement into categories. For incoming tides, a gain in water height of up to .40 foot per hour was categorized slow-moving, a gain of .41-.80 foot per hour was judged moderate, and a gain of .81 foot or more per hour was classified fast-moving. For outgoing tides, a loss in water height up to .50 foot per hour was categorized slow-moving, a loss of .51-1.0 foot per hour was designated moderate, and a loss of more than 1.0 foot per hour was considered fast-moving (outgoing tides in the survey had more rapid water movement than incoming tides). The number of tides in each category was approximately equal for valid comparison.

Once the categories were set up, a chart was made showing how many fish were seen per hour during each type of water movement:

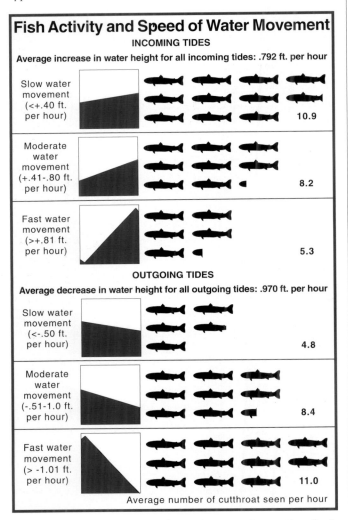

Fish Activity and Speed of Water Movement

INCOMING TIDES
Average increase in water height for all incoming tides: .792 ft. per hour

Slow water movement (<+.40 ft. per hour) — 10.9

Moderate water movement (+.41-.80 ft. per hour) — 8.2

Fast water movement (>+.81 ft. per hour) — 5.3

OUTGOING TIDES
Average decrease in water height for all outgoing tides: .970 ft. per hour

Slow water movement (<-.50 ft. per hour) — 4.8

Moderate water movement (-.51-1.0 ft. per hour) — 8.4

Fast water movement (> -1.01 ft. per hour) — 11.0

Average number of cutthroat seen per hour

This table produced perhaps the most interesting findings of the whole survey and the clearest indication of behavioral patterns among sea-run cutthroat: The slower the water movement during an incoming tide, the more fish were seen; conversely, the faster the water movement during an outgoing tide, the more fish were seen. The figures, in fact, are virtually mirror images of one another.

Why this should be so remains a mystery, but it does suggest that sea-run cutthroat respond to changes in the speed of tidal movement, and all other things being equal, anglers may expect to find more of them during a slow-moving incoming tide or a fast-moving outgoing tide. This finding partly confirmed one of my impressions, which had been that periods of rapid water movement always were best to fish; that turned out to be true at least for outgoing tides.

Other variables still had to be considered, among them water height and daily tidal range (the difference between low and high water). Either one of these, or both, might influence cutthroat behavior. So additional tables were set up to compare average water height and tidal range with fish-sighting data to determine if there was any correlation. The results indicated

there was not, leading to the conclusion that while water movement plays an extremely important role in cutthroat behavior, average water height and daily tidal range do not.

There is an important exception to this, however. Remembering the Washington Fly Fishing Club experiment at Dewatto Bay, which suggested that three feet of water over datum seemed to represent a threshold of comfort for sea-run cutthroat, I searched the observation data for all periods when the height of the tide was three feet or less. Observations made during those times yielded an average of only 1.6 fish seen per hour. This apparently confirms the notion that when the tide falls to a level of three feet or below, cutthroat become scarce. Presumably, under these circumstances, they leave the estuary and go elsewhere, probably into deeper water where they have more access to cover and food.

There remained some other calculations to be made. One was to compare average daily sightings by month to see if there were any variations in numbers of fish present.

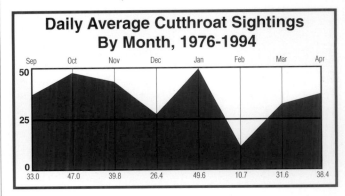

Daily Average Cutthroat Sightings By Month, 1976-1994

Sep	Oct	Nov	Dec	Jan	Feb	Mar	Apr
33.0	47.0	39.8	26.4	49.6	10.7	31.6	38.4

This graph shows that with the notable exceptions of December and February, especially the latter, there was a remarkable degree of consistency in numbers of cutthroat observed in the estuaries from September through April. It seems probable the drop-off in average daily sightings during December and February is because many cutthroat are spawning then. The catch of fresh-run kelts during those months, especially February, tends to confirm this observation.

I was also curious to see if there had been any significant changes in the numbers of cutthroat since I began making observations 18 years ago. Plotting the numbers on a graph provided the answer:

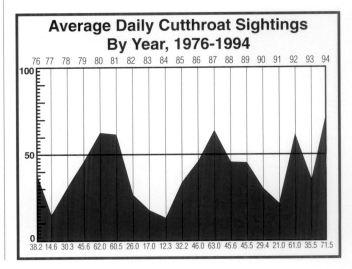

Average Daily Cutthroat Sightings By Year, 1976-1994

76	77	78	79	80	81	82	83	84	85	86	87	88	89	90	91	92	93	94
38.2	14.6	30.3	45.6	62.0	60.5	26.0	17.0	12.3	32.2	46.0	63.0	45.6	45.5	29.4	21.0	61.0	35.5	71.5

The Union River estuary, Washington, on a frozen winter morning.

The graph clearly shows some major fluctuations in cutthroat numbers over the years—or at least in the numbers of cutthroat I observed or caught during those years. It also shows a rather curious cyclical change in numbers, with steep declines about every seven years, followed in each case by a gradual recovery. Is this more than coincidence? Since the bulk of the sea-runs in Puget Sound and Hood Canal probably are three- or four-year old fish (two years of freshwater residence followed by one or two years spent partly or entirely in the estuaries), there is nothing in their life history to suggest their numbers should vary over a seven-year cycle, so it probably is nothing more than coincidence. But it would be interesting to compare these cycles with changes in weather patterns, ocean temperatures, or other external factors to see if there is any correlation. That, however, was beyond the means or scope of my experiment.

How should one evaluate all these findings? First, it should be remembered that these observations were confined to Puget Sound and Hood Canal and the results may not necessarily be valid for other estuarine environments. That's especially true in view of the many different life-history strategies employed by sea-run cutthroat populations over their vast range. It also bears repeating that the observations were limited to the eight months from September through April, and the patterns revealed may not necessarily hold during other months. Perhaps most important, this was not a scientifically controlled experiment, subject to the rigorous standards that ordinarily would be applied to such a test; it was merely one man's systematic long-term search for patterns in the behavior of sea-run cutthroat in the estuaries of Puget Sound and Hood Canal. Still, I am not aware of any other effort to observe the behavior of sea-run cutthroat over such a long period, and knowing how much care and diligence went into the observations and the analysis of the data, I am confident the results are of genuine value to anglers who fish the estuaries of Hood Canal and Puget Sound.

But the findings should not be regarded as Holy Writ; rather, I think the proper interpretation is to look upon them only as evidence of tendencies in sea-run cutthroat behavior. They appear to show that the movements of sea-run cutthroat are *not* completely random, that they *are* influenced by the daily pulses of the tide, that they *do* respond to tidal changes with some degree of consistency—but their responses are not as clear-cut, well-established or consistent as I had hoped they might turn out to be. Nevertheless, I believe these tendencies are useful to know.

The results also do not necessarily apply to other fish. Migrating salmon and steelhead and the marine species common to Northwest estuaries all show different patterns of behavior.

So what, then, is the answer to the age-old question of which tide is best to fish? Based on these findings—and if sea-run cutthroat are the primary quarry—then I think it is clear the middle two hours of a slow-moving incoming tide in the morning, or the middle two hours of a fast-moving outgoing tide that begins in the morning and carries over into the afternoon, are best.

There's an old adage, though, that the best time to go fishing is whenever you can get away. I don't expect to forget that, and neither should you.

VIII
SO MANY ESTUARIES, SO LITTLE TIME

There are many famous names in the language of fly fishing. Mention the Henry's Fork or the Madison, the Battenkill or the Babine, or any of a score or more of other well-known waters, and almost any fly fisher on the North American continent will instantly recognize the name. But so far there are no estuaries on that list of famous names.

Many anglers who have explored the potential of estuaries would just as soon keep it that way. Intimacy with estuaries and knowledge of the behavior of the fish that inhabit them usually comes only from spending countless days on the water, exploring, observing, trying new tactics, experimenting with new fly patterns, enduring all kinds of weather, through every season of the year. So the knowledge is hard-earned, and those who have earned it are entitled to treat it as something of value, not to be shared casually with those who have not paid a similar price. Most anglers who know the estuaries well also recognize their fragility and understand how easily they could be hurt by others who may not be as sensitive to such matters as they are. That's why most veteran estuary anglers are so protective of the things they know.

But this does present a practical problem for newcomers: If knowledge of the best times and places is so closely held, then how does one go about finding out where and when to fish the estuaries? The answer—unless you happen to know an experienced estuary fly fisher, and know him well enough to extract some of his hard-earned knowledge—is that you must find out for yourself. This may involve considerable time and effort, but for the most part the effort will be pleasant, and the time profitably spent. There are also some ways to shortcut the process. The best place to start is by obtaining the right kinds of maps and charts.

Maps and nautical charts

Maps describe the topography and shape of the land while nautical charts show the conformation and water depth along the coastline. Both are necessary tools for estuary anglers.

In the United States, navigation charts are published by the National Oceanic and Atmospheric Administration; in Canada, they are produced by the Hydrographic Service of the Department of Fisheries and Oceans. Traditionally, the publication format has been flat or rolled sheets, although some commercial publishers also offer atlases of bound charts. In addition, charts of some areas have recently become available on CD-ROM for use with personal computers—a good idea, perhaps, although a computer with a CD-ROM drive probably isn't something you would want to take with you in a small boat.

Charts in all these forms are sold in shops specializing in nautical equipment and publications, numbered and keyed to indices that make it easy to find the right ones for any particular area. They are not inexpensive, however, so anglers just getting started in estuary fishing are well advised to focus their attention on a small area to begin with, and buy only the charts needed for that area.

U.S. charts are published in scales starting at 1:20,000; these give the most detail and are the best to use for small-boat piloting, although they cover smaller areas than charts with higher scales. If you intend to use the charts for piloting, you should always obtain the latest available, regardless of scale, but if you're simply looking for likely places to fish, then the age of the chart doesn't matter very much. I once had a set of charts of Puget Sound and Hood Canal that were laminated in plastic for use as place mats on the dinner table; I would study them while eating, looking for places to fish, and I actually found some that way. I had no idea how old the charts were, but they were still adequate for that limited purpose. I wouldn't necessarily recommend this method, but it proves the point that if your intent is merely to look for places to fish, and you do not plan to use the charts for navigation, then almost any chart will do.

More and more estuaries are threatened by encroaching homes and summer cabins.

When studying a nautical chart for potential fishing places, you should begin by looking for small, protected bays and estuaries—if there's a freshwater tributary of any size, most charts will show it—that appear as if they might offer shelter from prevailing winds. Once you find such a spot, examine the depth soundings to determine the character of the water—whether it's deep or shallow, if it drops off quickly, or whether any shoals, sand bars, rock jetties, pilings, or other interesting features are indicated. NOAA's charts ease this process by showing tidal flats and marshes in green and shallow water in light blue so they are visible at a glance. The 1:20,000 charts also label bottom types, either by spelling them out—"mud," "sand," "gravel," etc.— or sometimes by abbreviation, such as RK for rocky bottoms, G for gravel, M for mud, Gr for grass, and S for sand.

Don't overlook lagoons with connections to salt water, even if they have no freshwater tributaries flowing into them. Brackish or saltwater lagoons are common along the Northern California and Oregon coasts, less common farther north. Sometimes they offer exciting angling opportunities, especially when inhabited by schools of baitfish that draw predatory gamefish to feed.

I know, for example, of one brackish lagoon draining into North Puget Sound that is regularly visited by schools of herring. A state biologist who discovered this fact decided to see what would happen if he stocked the lagoon with rainbow trout. The rainbow adapted easily to the brackish water and fed eagerly on the herring, and for several years the lagoon provided exceptional fishing for large, bright, resident rainbow trout for a few anglers in on the secret. This fishery, of course, was not completely "natural," but it illustrates the point: Lagoons are always worth trying.

Look also for estuaries with narrow entrances protected by sand spits, gravel bars, jetties, or other natural or artificial barriers. Fish often hold in the sheltered water behind such barriers waiting for food to be swept along by an incoming or outgoing tide, and this combination of circumstances can create ideal angling opportunities.

After you have identified several places that appear to meet these requirements, then it's time to consult maps of the adjacent landforms. There are several things to look for here, and perhaps the most important is access. The type of access depends on what fishing method is to be employed; if you plan to fish from a small, cartop boat, as I do most of the time, then the only access you need is a road next to the water. If you intend to wade along the beach, you won't need even that much; a road running close to the water will be enough, and you can hike the rest of the way. But if those are your only two choices, and there are no roads leading to the estuary you've pinpointed on the navigation chart, then it's probably time to look elsewhere.

Anglers with larger, longer-range boats, powered by motors and capable of traversing unprotected waters, may not face such limitations; an estuary inaccessible by land may be easily accessible from water, and in that case the map should be consulted for the nearest public ramp where a boat may be trailered and launched.

Topography is another important consideration. If you hope to find anadromous fish migrating through an estuary, then it's a good idea to study a topographic map to determine the gradient of the stream entering the estuary. If the stream flows in over a sheer 40-foot cliff, then obviously it is not going to have any migratory fish. Topography also

has an important bearing on access; the map may show a road leading to the estuary, but if it ends at the top of that same 40-foot cliff, then launching a small boat probably is going to be impossible.

Many maps also show the degree of settlement around a bay or estuary. If the area is thickly settled or developed, it may not be a place you care to fish. It also may mean that most of the waterfront is privately owned or controlled, and access may be limited or prohibited altogether. The magnitude of this problem cannot be exaggerated, especially in urban areas like Puget Sound and Southern British Columbia, where it grows worse all the time. The situation is especially bad in Washington, where the law not only allows private ownership of uplands, but also of tidelands in many cases, which limits access even more. Oregon, fortunately, had the foresight—or good luck—to designate its ocean beaches as public highways, so access to coastal estuaries there is not nearly as difficult.

The quadrangle maps published by the U.S. Geologic Survey or the Geological Survey of Canada are probably the best overall sources for the kind of information estuary anglers need. In the United States, privately published county maps also are often useful.

Once you've located a likely looking spot on a chart and confirmed the access on a map of the adjacent land, the next step is to go check it out. You will want to make

Brackish lagoons like the one in the foreground can provide unusual angling opportunities.

A wading angler fishes a small Hood Canal estuary at low tide.

certain you do this on a favorable tide, however, so it will be necessary to see what tides are predicted for the nearest primary or subordinate station on the day you plan to fish. The tide software mentioned in previous chapters is extremely useful for this purpose; any of these programs is far more flexible and versatile than a published tide table or calendar, and all of them offer the advantage of allowing users to print custom tables or graphs for almost any fishing location. The initial cost is certainly greater than the price of a tide calendar, but the software eliminates the need ever to buy another tide table or calendar, so it can save money over the long run.

Weather is the next consideration. Even the most sheltered estuaries are not immune from gale-force winds, or from discoloration due to flooded rivers. Those, of course, are extreme conditions, but if you're fishing an estuary for the first time you may discover that even a slight breeze from a particular direction is enough to make things difficult or dangerous. In any case, you should always try to get the latest and best weather information before heading out. Fortunately, this is much easier than it used to be.

Television and radio broadcasts are ready sources of weather information, but you can't always be certain the forecasts you hear are the latest available, and unless you live in a marine-oriented area, you will probably never hear a forecast specifically tailored for boaters or fishermen. Cable television weather channels, where available, are a somewhat better source; if you have the patience to watch long enough, you will often see a local marine weather forecast. Seattle and some other cities also have audiotex services where you can use a telephone to dial into a data base of recorded information, and these often provide late marine weather forecasts from government or private sources. Perhaps the best sources of all, however, are the continuous radio broadcasts from the National Weather Service, which can be received on portable radios set to a dedicated frequency. These battery-powered radios are sold in many electronics stores.

Sometimes even the latest and best weather information is ambiguous, and it's difficult to decide whether to go or wait and plan your trip another day; that's especially true if you're bound for an unfamiliar estuary, where you're not certain what to expect from the weather. When that's the

case, there's one final method I use to check the weather before I decide what to do: I step outside and look around. Since I live on the water, I can see what direction the wind is coming from and how strong it is; I can also see whether clouds are building on the horizon, what kind of clouds they are, and where they are headed. Even on winter mornings, when it's often too dark to see the water or the clouds, at least I can get some indication of wind strength by checking the limbs of the trees that grow around my house; if they are motionless, then I know the wind is calm, but if they are stirring vigorously it's a good indication the day may be too windy to fish. Such methods are far from infallible, of course, and not everyone lives in such an advantageous place as I do, but no matter where you live you can get some feeling for the weather just by going outside and looking around— and that will give you one more piece of information to help make your decision whether to go fishing.

I have not mentioned rain as a matter of importance. Rain is a matter of course in the Pacific Northwest, and during fall, winter, and spring months there are likely to be many more days with rain than days without it, so an angler who waits for a dry day may never go fishing at all. Dark, misty, rainy days also often work to a fisherman's advantage, bringing fish closer to the surface or into the shallows. So estuary anglers should plan to fish often in the rain, equip themselves accordingly, and perhaps even learn to enjoy it.

Sometimes, when you are exploring an unfamiliar estuary, even the best weather conditions and most favorable tides will not save you from frustration. You may reach a place you've identified on charts and maps only to find there is no public access after all, despite the roads shown on the maps, or you may find the place surrounded by summer homes and cabins not shown on the map. You may discover the estuary has the wrong type of bottom, despite what a navigation chart has indicated, and sometimes, even when everything else appears favorable, you may find the estuary holds no fish. On many days I have spent more time driving than fishing, steering my truck down narrow, rutted lanes in hopes of finding a glimpse of salt water at the other end, only to be frustrated time after time. I have seen "No Trespassing!" spelled every possible way—sometimes even correctly—and with every degree of emphasis; I have become an expert on the architecture of wooden and wire fences and locked gates of all kinds, and I have gotten stuck in mudholes on lonely roads far from any help. There have been more such episodes than I care to remember.

But there also have been occasions when I found exactly what I was looking for: A protected little bay with nothing but woods around its shores, a fair-sized stream running in, a convenient place to launch my little boat, and many willing fish. There are not many such places, and their numbers seem to grow fewer all the time, but if one is willing to invest the time and effort necessary to find them—and endure many frustrations in the process—then eventually success is bound to follow. When that happens, all the time and effort and frustration will seem worthwhile.

Ultimately you may locate a number of such places and learn which tides and weather conditions are best for each of them. You may also discover that some can be fished as easily from the beach as from a boat, or vice versa. And that brings up an important question: Which is better?

Wading vs. Boat Fishing

There are many ways to fish estuaries. You can wade along the beaches, fish from a small boat or canoe, or cast from a larger power boat capable of running in open water. Each method has advantages and disadvantages, and each requires acceptance of some important trade-offs. To a large extent the choice depends on where you live and what species of fish you plan to seek.

Waders are certainly the least expensive and most portable means of putting an angler within reach of estuarine fish, and in areas where public access is not a problem—along the Oregon Coast, for example, or on some of the more remote beaches of British Columbia and Southeast Alaska—they may offer the best solution. But that is usually not the case on places like Puget Sound or Hood Canal, where limited public access, especially over private tidelands, severely restricts the amount of water a wading angler can reach. Many tideland owners in these areas raise oyster crops which they guard jealously, and on a few occasions when I unwittingly waded into such waters, I have been confronted by angry, gun-toting property owners who thought I was an oyster poacher disguised as a fly fisherman. Another hazard is that some estuaries have very soft muddy bottoms, sometimes with patches of quicksand, so wading is sometimes dangerous.

But even in Puget Sound and Hood Canal, with their restricted access, there are some places where waders are perfectly adequate, and there are many such spots in other areas. This is especially true if one is planning to fish for migrating salmon or steelhead at a place where they swing close to shore, or if sea-run cutthroat are the target. Sea perch also may be found within casting distance of the shore, and sometimes even rockfish can be taken from a rock jetty or sea wall, especially during hours of darkness. Still, if you wade along the beaches there will undoubtedly be times when all the fish seem to be holding or surfacing just beyond the farthest distance you can cast from the deepest point you can wade—and those situations never fail to cause acute frustration. That is the risk an angler must accept if he or she chooses to stick with waders rather than some sort of floating craft.

These days, when floating craft are the subject, float tubes come most readily to mind. Tubes have become ubiquitous and anglers employ them for many different purposes, including some for which they definitely were not intended; the same is true for pontoon kickboats, which are becoming nearly as popular as float tubes. Unless you have a strong death wish, you should never think of using a float tube or kickboat for estuary fishing. Tides are the principal reason; even a slow-moving tide requires an angler in a tube or kickboat to keep his legs pumping continuously just to hold position, and no one can do that all day in cold sea

Wading sometimes is the best way to get at the water, especially if other means of access are limited.

water without getting dangerously tired. Even a slight increase in the speed of the tidal current or the strength of the wind may be more than a cold, weary, float-tube angler can cope with, and if the tide is on its way out, the trip to Japan is a very long one.

I say all this knowing that some anglers have used tubes or kickboats in estuaries and managed to get away with it—at least, I have yet to hear of any deaths resulting from their use. But I think it probably is only a matter of time until some hapless fisherman is swept away on an outgoing tide and overcome by exposure in the cold sea water. There may be places where tides are gentle enough and the water warm enough for tubes and kickboats to be used safely, but the estuaries of the Pacific Northwest are not among them. Even with an anchor to hold a tube or kickboat in place, it is far too dangerous to use these devices in estuaries; anglers who want to fish from a floating platform should choose something else.

Sea kayaks are certainly safe enough for this purpose; they are also easy to handle and, in experienced hands, capable of negotiating fairly open, windswept waters. The trade-off here is that it's impossible to stand up in a sea kayak, which limits an angler's ability to see rising or cruising fish or discern features on the bottom. Those are severe limitations. Canoes may be adequate for small waters, but the same limitation applies to many of them.

Jon boats or prams are a better choice for sheltered waters, so long as they are properly designed. By that I mean they should have flat bottoms, a gentle bow rise, a wide beam, and a high freeboard. That combination usually results in a stable platform that allows an angler to stand safely and cast in any direction. Small aluminum jon boats or prams are not prohibitively expensive. They are light in weight, can usually be carried on top of a car or truck, and they can be handled by a single person. They offer a choice of propulsion systems: oars, electric trolling motors, or low-horsepower outboard engines. Their disadvantages include limited range and an inability to tackle large, open bodies of water where strong winds and high waves are a possibility.

The other choice is something larger, usually an aluminum or fiberglass hull in the 14- to 18-foot class or even larger, matched to a suitably powered outboard. Except under extreme weather conditions, a boat of this size should be able to go almost anywhere in the estuaries; it should also offer enough stability for a pair of anglers to stand up and cast. The main drawback here is cost; such a boat usually has to be trailered, so one must buy and license a trailer as well as a boat—and then there is the additional expense of purchasing, maintaining, and operating a large outboard, which is considerable. Storage also can be a problem; you must have a place to park a trailered boat when it isn't in the water, and neighbors don't always appreciate having a boat parked on the street in front of your home. Finally, if one is seeking species such as sea-run cutthroat, which often feed very close to shore, a larger boat may have too much draft to get in close to the beach.

So there is no perfect solution—unless you have the means to invest in all these options, which few people do. Most anglers opt instead for what seems the best compromise. In my case, that means a small (9 1/4-foot) aluminum pram weighing 68 pounds. I can carry it on my truck, handle it easily by itself, and even carry it over short trails or through brush to a launching point if necessary. It's an extremely stable little boat that allows me to stand safely and cast in any direction. Sometimes I use an ancient, 4-horsepower outboard, but most of the time I row. Rowing is good exercise and I enjoy it, and as long as I am the only person in the boat, it moves easily and is extremely maneuverable. For a boat of its design, it also handles well in the wind. A single coat of paint is the only maintenance the pram has required in the more than 20 years I've owned it.

But the pram does have some disadvantages. With oars as the usual motive power, I can't go far in a single day, and sometimes it is difficult to row against a strong tide. I am also confined to well-protected waters, for the boat is too small to take into unsheltered reaches. It also is too small for more than one person to fish from, so if I go fishing with friends they must have their own craft. All these limitations can be irritating at times, but in years of searching the estuaries I've found a number of productive spots that are the right size and shape to cover easily and safely with my pram. It never hurts to hedge your bets, however, so I also carry a pair of waders, and if the wind gets too strong I can beach the boat and fish from shore.

The pram is a solution that works well most of the time, especially in the sheltered estuaries of Hood Canal and Puget Sound that I fish most often, but I would never advise anyone to take such a small boat—or a boat of any size, for that matter—into these waters without a good deal of boating experience. Even normally sheltered waters can become very dangerous in short order when the wind freshens, and a person without boat-handling experience in such conditions can get into trouble very quickly. So make this a rule of thumb, and follow it religiously: If the wind comes up, don't press your luck; get off the water as quickly as you can.

If you are not an experienced boater, you should go fishing with someone who is and spend some time learning the ropes before you go out alone, or in your own boat. It's also a good idea to attend one of the Coast-Guard approved boating classes offered in the United States and Canada.

Boating Equipment and Regulations

Whether or not you attend a boating class, you should at least familiarize yourself with Coast Guard equipment requirements and follow them. These requirements are not unreasonable or burdensome, and they were not estab-

A sign of the times: Access is becoming more and more difficult in urbanized areas like Puget Sound, Hood Canal, and Southern British Columbia.

lished just for fun; when you need something the Coast Guard requires you to have, you'll find you need it badly—and be very grateful you have it. Even if that need should never come, a Coast Guard citation for failing to comply with equipment regulations could cost you as much as $1,000.

In the United States, Coast Guard regulations require boats of 16 feet or less to carry a Type I, II, III, IV, or V personal flotation device for each person on board. These include wearable or inflatable life vests, jackets, and throwable life rings, but not boat cushions. Life jackets must be of appropriate size, and although they do not have to be worn while the boat is in operation, they must be "readily accessible"—meaning you should be able to reach one quickly in an emergency. Boats of more than 16 feet must carry one of these devices for each person aboard, plus an extra Type IV throwable life ring.

A boat of less than 16 feet without a motor also is required to carry a "portable dewatering device," which is bureaucratic language for a bailing can or scoop; a white light or lantern that must be displayed at night; and an anchor and line "of suitable size and length for the waters in which it is being operated." Anchors are essential for fly fishing in any case; when you locate a school of fish, you will need to anchor to keep the boat in position so you can cast. An anchor should have sufficient weight or strength to hold a boat in a strong tidal current; I use a 10-pound weight attached to a 3/8-inch line which is run through a clamp-on anchor release secured to the gunwhale.

There are additional equipment requirements for boats of more than 16 feet or any boat powered by motors. These are clearly detailed in a pamphlet, *Federal Requirements and Safety Tips for Recreational Boats*, available free from the U.S. Coast Guard. The pamphlet also outlines some of the basic "rules of the road" for boaters, and every boat owner should know these well. The U.S. Coast Guard also requires boats of any size "equipped with propulsion machinery" (including outboards) to be registered in the state of principal use and to display identification numbers on either side of its bow. The Coast Guard issues these numbers in Alaska; in Washington, Oregon, and California, the numbers are issued by the states.

Canadian Coast Guard equipment requirements are similar to those of the United States for boats less than 16 feet (5.5 meters under the metric system). They include an approved lifejacket, personal flotation device or boat cushion for each person on board; a pair of oars with rowlocks or two paddles; a hand-held bailer; lights as appropriate; and "some type of sound-signaling device," such as a hand-held air horn. These and additional requirements for larger boats or boats with motors are spelled out in an excellent publication, the *Safe Boating Guide*, available free from the Canadian Coast Guard. Federal registration in Canada applies only to boats powered by engines of 10 horsepower or more

In addition to those few items you are required to carry, there are plenty of others you should have along. Polarized glasses are an absolute necessity in any type of weather; without them your chances of seeing fish in the water are virtually nil, and your ability to see underwater obstructions or bottom features also will be limited. Other necessities include a hat large enough to provide good protection from

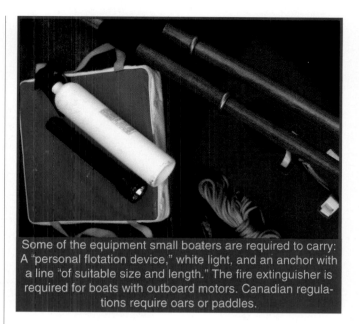

Some of the equipment small boaters are required to carry: A "personal flotation device," white light, and an anchor with a line "of suitable size and length." The fire extinguisher is required for boats with outboard motors. Canadian regulations require oars or paddles.

rain or sun (and one that won't come off easily in the wind), rain gear, calf-length watertight boots, heavy gloves, a flashlight with fresh batteries, waterproof matches, a small first-aid kit, sun block, a Swiss Army-type knife, and extra line for anchoring or mooring.

If you have a power boat, it's also good policy to take along tools and a few critical spare parts, such as extra cotter pins for an outboard-motor propeller. If you plan to go far, it's wise to carry a VHF radio and monitor the emergency Channel 16 (156.8 MHz), or carry a cellular phone if you're within range of cellular transmitters. Be certain to take compass, chart, and tide tables, and leave word where you're going and when you expect to return.

This may seem like a lot of gear and a lot of bother, but it's worth repeating that while you may never need some of these things, the time inevitably will come when you DO need at least one of them, and then you will need it urgently. Having it with you can make all the difference between a pleasant trip and disaster.

With a little preparation, planning, the proper equipment, and some experience operating small boats under a variety of weather and water conditions, you'll be ready to explore the estuaries. I say "explore" because that is mostly what you will be doing, going where few anglers have gone before, trying new places and new methods, pushing the envelope of your personal fly-fishing knowledge. No other area of the sport offers such opportunities for discovery.

Some days you will find fish and some days you will not, but there are always so many interesting things to see in estuaries that even on fishless days you will feel you have been denied nothing. Rare is the angler who can resist the captivating charms of an estuary, with all its infinite variety of sights and sounds and scents, and simply being there among all the estuary's teeming life is usually reward enough for anyone—so that when a fish does take your fly, as one surely will, you will feel doubly blessed, as if you had received more than your fair share of the best the world can offer.

So get ready. There are so many estuaries, and you have so little time.

This is the part of the book where you normally expect the author to say something like, "If I had to choose only one outfit to fish the estuaries, it would be . . . . " You will not read that here, for I could never be satisfied with only a single outfit for estuary fishing.

That is not to say that lots of elaborate or expensive tackle is necessary for this type of fishing; quite the contrary. Yet the minimum requirement is two complete outfits—one for a sinking line, the other for a floater. It is possible to switch back and forth and use only a single rod for both lines, but that would take unnecessary time away from fishing and involve other compromises I regard as unacceptable. Hence two outfits are the minimum.

The size of rod and weight of line are mostly a matter of personal preference, although one must give some consideration to the size and strength of fish he or she is likely to catch. My choice for wet-fly fishing in the estuaries is an 8 1/2-foot graphite rod matched to a 7-weight line with a weight-forward taper. This outfit is heavier than needed for sea-run cut-throat, the species I catch most often, but since one never knows exactly what size fish may take his fly in an estuary, the heavier rod gives some added insurance. I know, for example, that it is adequate to handle big, angry, chum salmon, ocean-bright winter steelhead, or heavy chinook salmon, which are likely to be the largest and strongest fish I will encounter in estuaries. The rod also is stout enough to cast the larger flies sometimes needed in this fishing. I rarely use flies longer than three inches, but even some of that size are bulky in design and offer lots of wind resistance, and a strong rod is needed to throw them well. I know other anglers who routinely use flies up to six inches in length, especially when fishing for salmon, and some of these patterns may require the use of an even heavier rod.

My favorite line is an intermediate mono-core, sometimes called a "Slime Line." I like this line for its versatility; by varying the amount of time I allow it to sink after each cast, I can easily change the depth at which I am fishing;

and since I most often fish in shallow water, I rarely need a faster-sinking line. The line is not without disadvantages, however; on cold winter mornings it stubbornly retains its "memory," falling to the bottom of the boat in a bird's nest of tight coils, and repeated stretching is necessary to get it in casting shape. Another problem is that an unusually strong tidal flow may prevent the line from sinking to the desired depth; when that happens, a faster-sinking wet-tip or full-sinking line sometimes offers a better solution, although a strong tidal flow makes it difficult to hook fish regardless what type of line is used. A wet-tip or full-sinking line also is best for working deeper water.

Behind the line I attach 100 yards of 18-pound-test backing to the reel. More backing would not be out of place, but that is the maximum capacity of the reel I use most of the time; there have been occasions when it was barely enough. At the business end of the line I attach a short leader tapered steeply down to a tippet with 6-pound breaking strength. The short leader keeps the fly at the same depth as the line, and the tippet strength seems a good compromise between usual water clarity and fish size. However, it's not strong enough for big winter steelhead or chum salmon, and when I find myself with a chance to catch one of these I change to an 8- or 10-pound tippet.

For floating-line work I use a very light 7 1/2-foot graphite rod matched to a 6-weight line of either weight-forward or double-taper design (the former allows a little more distance). While it is possible, and sometimes desirable, to fish a wet fly on a floating line, I use this outfit for dry-fly fishing most of the time. It is well matched in size and strength to the sea-run cutthroat and resident coho salmon that are my most frequent quarry, but not strong enough to handle larger sea-run salmon or steelhead—and while these fish don't often rise to a dry fly in salt water, they do sometimes. When that happens, the encounter usually is brief and ends in favor of the fish, but I so much enjoy using the light outfit on smaller fish that I am perfectly willing to accept the occasional loss of a larger one.

A sea-run cutthroat that hit a Cutthroat Candy dry fly.

The floating line is attached to 50 yards of backing on the reel. At the other end is a leader of at least nine feet tapered to a 3-pound-test tippet. The water in most of the estuaries I fish is extraordinarily clear, and although estuarine fish ordinarily are not leader shy, the clarity of the water seems to indicate a leader of about that length and breaking strength.

Of all the tackle used in estuary fly fishing, the reel is most susceptible to damage from saltwater corrosion, so I always choose reels with the fewest moving parts. For many years my wet-fly reel has been an old Ocean City model with a friction drag and no click; it was owned by my father and has been in steady use for more than 60 years, but still is going strong; its only battle scars are a few spots of rust on the reel seat. It has proved its worth time after time in memorable battles with big fish, and my only regret is that it lacks a click, so all those battles were fought in silence.

The longevity of this reel is explained by my habit of keeping it clean and well lubricated both inside and out. I regularly coat the shaft with oil and apply grease to the end of the spindle, where it fits into the spool, and spray the whole outside casing with fine oil. The reel probably is good for many more years of wear, but I plan to retire it soon in recognition of its long and faithful service, and replace it with a reel that has a loud click.

The reel I use with a floating line is also simple in design, configured in the opposite fashion from my wet-fly reel: it has a click but no drag, except for rim control. This works fine because most of the fish I hook on dry flies do not require a drag. As with the old Ocean City reel, I keep this one well lubricated, and it has yet to show a serious sign of wear after more than a decade of use.

When I began fishing estuaries, I was very careful to rinse my equipment in fresh water after each day's fishing, even stripping the line from the reel and bathing it in a sink full of fresh water. That was a lot of trouble, however, and I soon got out of the habit. Now I simply wipe down my rods with a clean cloth before putting them away, always taking care to be certain the guides and other hardware are free of moisture. But that's all I do, and my equipment does not seem to have suffered because of it.

Flies are a different story. Once a fly is used in salt water, it should be dried out completely before it is put away in a box—and then it should be placed in a box by itself, or one that does not contain any unused flies. Rust is the reason; most hooks rust quickly after immersion in salt water, even those coated or plated to resist corrosion, especially if some of the plating has been removed in the process of sharpening the hook. Even stainless-steel hooks are not completely immune; the hooks themselves may not rust, but if the materials of the fly have been saturated with salt water they can spread corrosion to other flies. A single spot of rust is like a bad apple in a barrel; it will spread and ruin every other fly in the box. Sometimes a fly tied on a plated hook may be fished two or three times before the hook starts to show signs of corrosion, but you should expect any fly used in salt water to have a short life. If you fish estuaries often, you'll be tying plenty of flies.

For obvious reasons, plastic or Styrofoam boxes are better than metal containers for saltwater flies.

A dry fly floats over an oyster bed. Dry-fly fishing is deadly for sea-run cutthroat in estuaries.

Other equipment needed for estuary fishing is similar to that needed for any type of fly fishing: A vest or tackle bag to carry fly boxes, reels, and spools of leader material; a set of clippers; a hook sharpener; a set of forceps to remove hooks from fish; and a pair of pliers to pinch down the barbs of hooks. Polarized glasses, already mentioned, are an absolute necessity. A landing net is optional—if you can release a fish without netting it, so much the better for the fish—but if you are fishing for adult salmon or steelhead, then a net will make life much easier both for you and the fish.

Doubtless you'll think of many other items without any help from me. But whatever you choose to carry with you while fishing the estuaries, remember this: Always take good care of your equipment, and it will always take good care of you.

Tactics

While specific tactics are often necessary for individual species of fish, some estuary fly-fishing techniques are almost generic. It seems best to start with these—beginning with wading.

Simply because you're wearing a pair of waders doesn't mean you should always get them wet, especially if you are fishing for species like sea-run cutthroat or sea perch that sometimes feed close to shore. In these circumstances, it's often better to stay out of the water and cast from land. The importance of recognizing when to wade and when to stay out of the water cannot be overemphasized. I've lost track of how many times I've seen anglers wade into places they should have been fishing, usually with predictable results: they caught nothing, and neither did anyone fishing near them.

So before entering the water, always take time to case things out. Put on polarized glasses and examine the water for signs of fish; if the light is good and the water clear enough, you may be able to see a school of perch huddled up against the shore, or the flash of a feeding cutthroat. If you see nothing in the water, then watch for rises or "nervous water" on the surface—subtle bulges, ripples, or any slight disturbance that might conceivably be caused by the movement of a fish. If you still see nothing, then trust your instinct; if it tells you fish are there, they probably are. Even when there is nothing at all to suggest that fish are feeding close in, it's a good idea to make the first few casts from shore, testing the water before you wade into it.

Whether you stay on the beach or wade out into the water, your casts should always be in the direction of the tide. For example, if the tide is flowing from your right to your left, you should cast to the left; this way the current will keep your line taut so it will be easier to detect a strike and set the hook. Your first casts should parallel the beach close in; if they produce nothing, then quarter outward from the beach until the movement of the tide begins to form a belly in your line. At that point, if no fish have moved to your fly, it's time to move down the beach and start the process over again.

On most occasions, the tide will not be flowing neatly from your right to left, or vice versa; often it will be moving at some angle to your position, or even going directly away or coming directly toward you. The key is to establish the direction of movement and try to use it to your advantage. Ordinarily you can do this unless the tide is flowing directly toward you; then usually the only option is retrieve your fly as quickly as possible to keep the current from forming an impossible amount of slack in your line.

One common mistake anglers make in estuary fishing is to cast out too far, particularly when the target species is sea-run cutthroat, sea perch, or any other fish that feeds close to the beach. It's worth repeating that you should always fish the shallows close to the beach before you think about casting farther out.

Stripping baskets are an enormous convenience for wading anglers. Worn around the waist, they provide handy storage for line stripped in after each cast; they also make the next cast easier. Without a stripping basket, it's easy for loose coils of fly line to blow around in the wind or otherwise get away and tangle around oyster shells, snags, or other flotsam, and an angler can end up spending more time freeing his line than fishing. A stripping basket will prevent that; it's a small investment that quickly pays for itself in convenience.

It's also important to check the water first before you begin fishing from a boat. If you're running the boat under power, cut the motor before you reach the spot you plan to fish and edge up to it as quietly as possible, preferably without using the motor at all. Take care not to run the boat into the water you should be fishing, and when you get close, ease the anchor overboard and take a long look at the water ahead. Watch for any signs of fish; if you see them, start casting. If not, it's still a good idea to explore the water with a pattern of casts before moving in closer.

Here again you should cast in the direction of the tide, taking care not to allow the current to form a belly in your line. If nothing moves to your fly, lift anchor, move down the beach, re-anchor, and try again. By hop scotching along the beach in this fashion, you will have a good chance of finding fish sooner or later. It also pays to remember that many estuarine species move around rapidly, so even if an area has been checked once and found devoid of fish, it may be worth returning to check again later; on the second try, you may find it teeming with fish.

This method of exploring the water obviously calls for a lot of raising and lowering of anchors, and you should have a system that allows you to do this with a minimum of fuss and effort. Larger boats usually have some sort of pulley system built in for this purpose, but smaller cartop boats do not. Herter's, the now-defunct outdoor mail-order catalog company, once sold clamp-on anchor releases that were a godsend to small-boat fishermen. They consisted of a pulley-and-check assembly bolted to a clamp that fit over the gunwhale of a boat. The clamp could be tightened easily with a thumbscrew to hold the device securely in place, and the anchor rope was then threaded through the pulley-and-check assembly. All the angler had to do was to pull up on the rope to release the check and either raise or lower the anchor. I purchased two of these devices, which have since rusted to the point they are virtually unrecognizable, and to my knowledge they are no longer made anywhere. So I made one of my own using a pulley-and-check assembly originally designed to be bolted permanently to a boat's deck. This I attached to a clamp designed as part of a trolling rod holder. Like the old Herter's device, the clamp is large enough to fit over the gunwhale of my boat and tightens

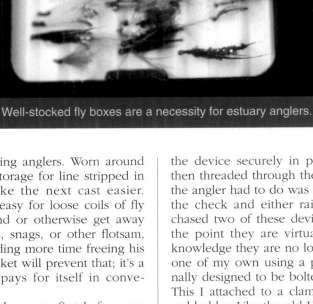
Well-stocked fly boxes are a necessity for estuary anglers.

Tangled growths of saltwort or pickleweed near the high-tide line are favorite haunts of feeding sea-run cutthroat at high water.

with a thumbscrew. The resulting gadget is not as rugged as the Herter's design, but it works just as well—and the parts cost less than $10.

The anchor itself should be able to hold the boat in position against a strong tidal flow and a brisk wind, which means it must have plenty of weight or a method of gripping the bottom. But even the best anchor won't hold if you don't let out enough line—usually a length equivalent to at least two or three times the depth of the water (the Canadian Coast Guard recommends five times the water depth). This extra length or "scope" of line helps keep your boat firmly anchored even in a strong tidal current or brisk wind.

Why bother with all this? If you are fly fishing from a boat, you *must* be able to anchor when you find a school of feeding fish; otherwise the tide will sweep you quickly beyond casting range.

Incidentally, the U.S. Coast Guard strongly advises boaters to anchor from the bow, never from the stern. The reason is that most boats have more freeboard in the bow than the stern, and dropping the anchor from a narrow stern transom in a strong tide could pull the transom under water and swamp the boat.

Once an angler is in position and casting in the direction of the tide, what he or she does next depends on the type of line and fly being used. If an intermediate or slow-sinking line is being used, then the angler must decide how long to let it sink before starting the retrieve. This obviously depends on the water depth and species of fish being sought, but if one is simply searching the water for whatever might be there, then it may be advisable to make several casts in each direction and let the fly sink to various depths before starting the retrieve. This way it is possible to explore the water vertically as well as horizontally.

Sometimes there will be no choice except to cast across the tide or at an angle to its flow, so that the current seizes the line and begins to form a belly in it. That makes it much more difficult to detect a strike or set the hook, but there are a couple of ways to minimize the problem. One is to keep a close eye on the line and follow its movement with the rod tip so the rod is always pointed straight toward the fly; this will reduce the size of the belly in the line. Another way is to make shorter casts so there is less line for the tide to work on.

With a floating line, the wind becomes as much a factor as the tide, sometimes more. In an ideal situation, the wind and tide will be moving in the same direction so it is possible for an angler to cast with both behind him. That seldom happens in reality, however; more often the tide will be going one way and the wind another. Then you must determine which is stronger; if the wind is stronger,

Sea-run cutthroat are among the last wild trout in the Pacific Northwest, just one of many reasons why they should be released.

cast in its direction, and vice versa. The object is to try to keep the stronger force from forming a belly in your floating line.

Again, there will be situations when you have no choice except to cast across tide. The same techniques used to keep a belly from forming in a sinking line will work with a floating line, with one important addition: You can also mend a floating line to prevent a belly from forming, or to minimize the size of one that does form.

How you retrieve the fly depends on what type of fly it is and what species of fish you're seeking. If the fly is a baitfish imitation fished on a sinking line, then rapid, erratic pulls make a good generic retrieve. This means three or four quick, short pulls, followed by a brief pause, then another couple of quick pulls, another pause, and so on—always randomly varying the number of pulls and the number and duration of pauses between pulls. This type of retrieve always has produced good results for me, particularly in searching situations.

Flies intended to imitate shrimp, amphipods, or pill-bugs obviously require a different sort of movement—usually a slow, patient retrieve, perhaps interspersed with an occasional quick pull.

With floating flies, motion is the key. You can cast a dry fly, let it sit for a long time, and usually nothing will happen—but if you begin skating it over the surface so it leaves a little V-shaped wake, then there's no telling what may grab it, although cutthroat and resident coho are the most likely candidates. Color and shape do not seem to matter very much; what makes a dry fly successful in estuaries is its ability to float and create a disturbance when skated over the surface. With this method, casting in the direction of the wind or tide is even more critical, for a dry fly should always be retrieved against the direction of strongest water movement. This way it encounters more water resistance, which helps the fly float better; it also creates more surface disturbance to attract the attention of fish. A dry fly retrieved in the same direction as the wind or tide usually sinks easily—and even if it doesn't, it causes less surface disturbance.

On occasion, when sea-run cutthroat or resident coho were rising well, I have had them come to a floating fly fished with a dead drift, taking it with head-and-tail rises just like trout rising to mayflies in a stream. This is always exciting to see and I enjoy it when it happens, but most of the time a dry fly fished on a dead drift will not work in the estuaries and it will take a skated fly to bring fish to the surface.

It is common for fish to rise to a skated dry fly without taking it, or without taking it firmly. That's because not all rises are "taking" rises; sometimes cutthroat respond to a skated dry fly in estuaries much as summer steelhead often do in rivers: they bump the fly with their noses, jump over it, splash around it, chase it in a rising wave of water, or do almost anything except open their mouths and take it. These playful rises—if that's what they are—can be exciting to watch, but also quite frustrating. Sometimes changing the speed of the retrieve—either speeding it up or slowing it down—will result in taking rises.

The very fact that the dry fly must nearly always be in motion also makes it more difficult to hook rising fish. The timing of the strike is critical and it takes experience to get the hang of it. With sea-run cutthroat, it's often necessary to wait for the fish to start down with the fly in its mouth before trying to set the hook; if you strike too soon you will feel nothing. But an angler's usual impulse is to strike as quickly as possible, and waiting for the fish to turn down requires extreme patience. Cutthroat also may respond differently from one day to the next, so each new day of fishing can require an adjustment in timing. Suffice it to say, you'll have many more rises than hook-ups while fishing dry flies in estuaries.

You should also be prepared to change tactics when you encounter different species. Here's an idea of what to expect from the most common species of Pacific Northwest estuaries:

COHO SALMON

Seasons

Migrating sea-run adults begin showing up in the waters of Southeast Alaska and British Columbia in late April or early May, although usually it is August before they become readily available in large numbers to fly fishers. August and September are the best months for these fish in Washington and Oregon waters, but final-stage returning adults may be found in inner estuaries from late September through early November. Resident coho in Puget Sound and Hood Canal are planted in late fall and begin entering anglers' catches within a few weeks; they are available almost year-around.

Water Type

Migrating adults often swing close to shore, especially off points reaching out into deeper water, and sometimes come within casting range of the beach. They are also found in open waters. They are most easily seen when they reach the inner estuaries, near the mouths of the

Wall-to-wall oysters in a bay along British Columbia's Sechelt Peninsula. Oyster beds are prime places to find sea-run cutthroat.

streams for which they are headed; here their arrival is marked by the sight of schools of leaping and rolling fish.

Young resident "feeder" coho are often found mingled with schools of sea-run cutthroat along rocky or gravel beaches in the estuaries, especially on overcast or dark days. On bright days, they move into deeper, open water, but even then sometimes feed close to the surface, usually along tide lines or rips.

Tides

When salmon are feeding in open water, the state of tide may not be important, except in how it forms or affects rips where food may be present. But tides are critical when salmon enter shallow water, especially when adult sea-run coho move into the inner estuaries. These fish often congregate in deeper holes at high tide, usually in schools with many leaping or porpoising fish visible; some fish may stray from deeper holes into the shallows. At the final stage of their migration, these fish appear to follow the tides in and out, waiting for a rise of water in their home river before beginning their ascent. They dash in on the high tide and depart just as quickly when it ebbs, and the best time for an angler to find them is on a rising tide or during high-water slack. At this stage of their migration, few of these fish are disposed to feed; only the odd one can be provoked into striking, so an angler's odds of success are directly proportional to the number of fish present.

Tactics

For migrating adults, sinking lines and wet flies are best; in open waters, particularly on bright days, an extra fast-sinking line may be necessary to reach fish. A rapid, erratic retrieve, like that described earlier, sometimes works; at other times, it may be necessary to strip the fly as fast as humanly possible. It's best to vary the speed and type of retrieve until you find what works.

Resident coho feeding in the inner estuaries from December through May respond well to skated dry flies or small baitfish, shrimp, or amphipod imitations fished on intermediate or slow-sinking lines. Later in the year, when they begin their "mini-migrations," slightly larger baitfish imitations may be in order.

Charlie Walkinshaw plays a sea-run cutthroat in Hood Canal while his father, Walt, records the action on film.

Fly Patterns

Migrating coho far from their rivers of origin and still actively feeding may be taken on any number of baitfish or shrimp imitations. Once they get close to their home rivers and cease feeding, their interest usually can be stimulated only by "attractor" flies in colors of fluorescent orange or chartreuse. However, bright salmon near the mouths of their home rivers may still sometimes be taken on baitfish patterns.

Scores of fly patterns have been developed for coho and other species of Pacific salmon and there is great similarity among many of them, especially baitfish imitations; most have bodies of silver mylar or tinsel, hair wings of blue, green, and white or a combination of all these, and often some sort of added flash from synthetic materials. Many anglers tie their own, but those who buy flies would be well advised to ask for versions of the Deceiver, a generic baitfish imitation originally developed on the East Coast which has made a successful transition to Western waters.

Other useful coho patterns include Lambuth's Candlefish, other generic candlefish and sand lance imitations, and small euphasid shrimp or amphipod patterns, such as any of the many Pink Shrimp variations or the Golden Shrimp.

For adult cohos at the final stage of their migration, when all feeding has ceased, bright patterns such as Randy's Retiary or the Chum Candy (which also works for coho despite its name) are effective at times.

For small resident "feeder" coho along the beaches or in open water, a skated Cutthroat Candy or similar dry fly is usually deadly, although any high-floating fly will work if kept afloat and in motion. Wet patterns include the same shrimp or amphipod imitations already mentioned, and these are particularly effective during winter months. Smaller baitfish imitations like the Tarboo Special, Fry Fly, or any number of similar patterns also may work, especially during spring and summer. The Knudson's Spider is a good traditional attractor pattern for winter fishing.

(Dressings for these and other fly patterns mentioned in this chapter will be found in the appendix.)

CHUM SALMON

Seasons

Chum salmon are available to anglers only during the final stages of their migration. In Southeast Alaska that may be as early as September; farther south it is progressively later. The popular chum fisheries in Washington's Hood Canal reach their peak in November, but some runs continue into December or even early January.

Water Type

Look for large schools of adult chum salmon in shallow water off beaches near the mouths of rivers or in the deeper channels formed where a river drains into salt water.

Tides

These fish are anxious to get upstream and the tide doesn't seem to matter much to them; they will gather off the mouths of rivers at any stage of tide. This is also where they are sought by most anglers, and the number of fishermen may be almost as great as the number of chum milling around in front of them. I prefer to avoid such mob scenes and instead do most of my chum fishing along beaches far from any river. Low tides are best for this; the chum schools are more readily visible at this stage of tide, especially along gently sloping beaches, although they may be wary and difficult to approach.

Tactics

These vary with the mood of the fish. Again, it's important to remember that at this stage of their lives, the chum are not feeding and must be provoked into striking. Hundreds of fish may be packed into a single school, and of all these only a few can ever be persuaded to take, so this is another situation where chances of success are directly proportional to the number of fish present. In fishing over a dense school off a river mouth, an intermediate or wet-tip line retrieved very slowly seems to work best, although sometimes no retrieve at all is even better. The technique in the latter case is simply to let the fly drift with the tide.

Fishing for schools along beaches away from rivers requires a different approach. In most cases the schools are not nearly as large as those found off river mouths, so an angler's chances of success are reduced dramatically—but at least it's possible to fish without shoulder-to-shoulder angling mob scenes. At low tide these schools may be found by the disturbances they create in the shallows—usually a host of watery arrows moving rapidly in the same direction. The schools are most easily followed by boat, and the usual fishing technique is to try to get ahead of a moving school, cast in front of it, and wait for the fish to arrive before imparting any action to the fly—and then only a very slow retrieve is advised.

The fish in these schools are very nervous in the shallows and spook easily, so it's hard to get close to them in daylight. But they are easily approached after dark in areas where it is legal to fish for them at such times. The best technique then is simply to cast from the beach and wait for results; chum salmon also seem far more willing to take a fly during hours of darkness than in daylight.

Fly Patterns

The most consistently effective patterns for chum salmon are chartreuse or green in color, with hot pink a fairly close runner-up. Suggested wet flies include the Chum Candy, lime-green Woolly Bugger, Green Weenie, and Alaskabou.

Some anglers use patterns incorporating glow-in-the-dark Flashabou for night fishing. This material is exposed to a flashlight or lantern beam after every few casts to make sure it continues to glow brightly. This is effective, although questions have been raised about the ethics of using such materials.

I have heard reports of chum salmon being taken in Alaskan waters on a very large skated dry fly with the improbable name of Pink Polliwog. I have tried this pattern on chum salmon in Washington waters, so far without success, but the idea of taking chum on a dry fly is so attractive that I plan to keep trying.

PINK SALMON

Seasons

Like the chum, pink salmon become available to anglers only as adults near the end of their migration. They are encountered annually as early as April in the open waters of Southeast Alaska and British Columbia, but do not come within reach of beach casters until much later—usually late June through early August in Southeast Alaskan waters, late July through August in British Columbia. In Washington waters, September is the prime month, but runs occur only in odd-numbered years.

Water Types

Points and rocky beaches lying along migratory routes, or inner estuaries at the final stage of the salmon's migration, are the best places to find pinks.

Tides

Pink salmon in the final stages of migration behave a lot like chum; they are anxious to get upstream, and tides don't seem to matter much. Like chum, they travel in schools, often easily detected by the sight of porpoising, rolling, or leaping fish. As with chum, these schools are most readily visible at low tide, roaming up and down shallow beaches somewhere in the vicinity of their home river.

Tactics

Pink salmon occasionally seem more willing to take a fly than any other adult Pacific salmon, but that is not to say they are eager. Again, it's a matter of numbers; the more pinks available, the better one's chances of finding one or two willing to take. Most fishing is done from the beach or from small boats in shallow water. Intermediate,

Autumn sunlight sparkles from the water of a small estuary on northern Hood Canal.

slow-sinking, or wet-tip lines are used with wet flies, and a slow retrieve seems best. Pink salmon schooled up in shallow water are extremely wary and spook easily, so they must be approached with caution, especially in a boat.

Pink salmon in salt water have unusually soft mouths, so a delicate hand is required to set the hook. Too swift or too strong a reaction may only succeed in pulling the hook out of the fish.

Fly Patterns

As befits their name, pink salmon seem to prefer almost anything pink—the brighter, the better. Suggested patterns include Barry Thornton's Pink Eve and the Humpy Hooker.

CHINOOK SALMON

Seasons

Mature chinook salmon returning from their ocean migrations come within easy reach of fly fishers only when they enter the shallow water of the estuaries at the end of their journey. There is wide variety in the timing of these migrations among different stocks, and some runs—especially those of spring and summer—are too small or spread out over too much time to provide practical fisheries. The best runs seem to be those of early fall; they tend to have the largest numbers of fish and the most discrete timing. In Alaskan waters, these runs may peak as early as September, with progressively later runs farther south. October is prime time in Washington and Oregon waters.

In waters with populations of resident chinook, or "blackmouth" as they are called in Puget Sound, fish are available virtually year-around.

Water Types

Fall-run adult chinook frequently congregate in deeper holes when they reach the inner estuaries. Resident chinook inhabit deeper, open waters most of the time but occasionally come close to the surface on dark, overcast days.

Tides

Adult chinook near the end of their migration behave much like coho; they enter the inner estuaries on a rising tide, then head out again when the tide begins to ebb, repeating the process while they wait for a freshet that will allow them to ascend their home river. When present in the inner estuaries, they usually roll and porpoise like other salmon, although perhaps not quite so readily.

Since resident chinook often feed in deeper, open water, they are accessible to anglers on any stage of tide.

Even in winter, when the trout streams of sunshine fishermen are running dark and cold, there are steelhead and cutthroat moving in the estuaries.

A pair of anglers fishing for coho salmon near a creekmouth in Vaughn Bay, Puget Sound.

Tactics

Precocious males or "jack" chinook are easiest to take on flies, and usually there are a fair number of these smaller fish among schools of returning adults. With larger adult fish, it's another numbers game; few are willing to take, so the more fish present, the better an angler's chance of hooking one. Sinking lines and wet flies, usually fished with an extremely rapid retrieve, are needed to entice these fish.

Resident chinook ordinarily can be reached only by very fast sinking lines cast into deep, open water, but on occasions when they are feeding close to the surface, a slower-sinking line may do the job. Fly patterns and retrieves should be matched to whatever the fish are taking—usually baitfish or shrimp.

Fly Patterns

To the extent they have a preference at all, sea-run chinook in the inner estuaries sometimes respond to hot-orange flies, like the Retiary or any similar pattern, retrieved very rapidly. Resident chinook can be taken on baitfish patterns such as the Deceiver, Lambuth's Candlefish and others, sand lance imitations, or pink shrimp patterns.

SEA-RUN CUTTHROAT

Seasons

July through September from Northern California to Willapa Bay in Washington; also in North Puget Sound and other northern estuaries fed by large river systems; year-round in South Puget Sound, Hood Canal, British Columbia's Sechelt Peninsula, and other sheltered estuaries fed primarily by small streams.

Water Types

Sea-run cutthroat display a marked preference for rocky, cobbled bottoms and shallow bays rimmed by patches of saltwort or pickleweed; here they find friendly habitat for the amphipods and isopods that form such an important part of their saltwater diet. They also frequently gather over oyster beds, although their reason for doing so is not readily apparent. One theory is that they use oyster beds for cover. This may seem odd, given that when oyster beds are fully exposed or covered only by shallow water at low tide, they gleam whitely and appear devoid of cover. But when covered by three feet of water or more, the light reaching them is less intense and the irregularly shaped shells break it up and scatter it in alternating patterns of brightness and shadow; under these conditions, it's easy for a cutthroat to hide in the broken patterns of darkness and light.

Sea-runs in salt water also are very site-specific in their behavior. That is, once they find a place to their liking, they will return to it again and again to feed. Since their schools are nearly always in motion, they may visit such places for only a short time before moving on to the next one, but if an angler discovers one of these spots, he or she may return to it with confidence that fish are bound to appear sooner or later.

Often there is nothing obvious about these places that sets them apart from their surroundings, and it is always puzzling why cutthroat will gather in one place and not another. The answer may have to do with tidal currents and how they are influenced by the local topography. A gentle rise in the bottom may cause the tide to flow more swiftly over that spot, perhaps concentrating more food in the area; conversely, a dip or swale in the bottom may slow the tidal current, trapping food in an eddy or making it easier for fish to hold against the flow. These things can be very subtle and difficult to observe.

As much as they like to return to the same places, sea-runs also habitually avoid some types of habitat. In many years of fishing for sea-run cutthroat, I have found them only rarely over muddy or sandy bottoms or along clam beaches. Obviously cutthroat must sometimes pass through such areas to reach their preferred habitats, but they do not stay long and are never found consistently in these places.

Cutthroat also are often found around old pilings, floats, or other structures.

Tides

As indicated in Chapter VII, the best tides are the middle two hours of a slow-moving incoming morning tide or the middle two hours of a fast-moving outgoing tide in the middle of the day. An ideal situation is to find cut-

A row of old pilings creates a surrealistic scene on Chuckanut Bay, Washington.

throat lying in wait for food being swept over a shallow gravel bar by a swift-moving outgoing tide. However, at least a few cutthroat usually can be found at almost any stage of tide when the water is three feet or more above datum.

Tactics

Examine the water carefully for signs of rising or jumping cutthroat. A jumping fish is always easy to see, but the rise of a sea-run cutthroat is often subtle—nothing more than the fleeting slice of a dorsal fin through the surface, leaving only a slight disturbance in its wake. It takes experience to recognize and identify these discreet rises.

It is not clear why cutthroat rise in salt water when insects are so rarely present on the surface. Very few species of insects hatch in saltwater, and most of those species are found in the tropics, so saltwater hatches appear to have little or nothing to do with the cutthroat's propensity to rise. However, there are occasions when mayflies hatching on a nearby river may be blown onto an estuary in sufficient numbers to set off a rise of trout; more commonly, flights of carpenter ants or termites will emerge from the woods surrounding an estuary and fall to the water, triggering a vigorous rise. When any of these happens, an appropriate floating imitation is very much in order. Under most circumstances, however, there will be nothing visible on the surface to stimulate cutthroat to rise. We can only be thankful that they rise anyway, and take advantage of the phenomenon by giving them a target—our own dry fly.

If cutthroat are rising, then it is vital to try to cover each rise as quickly as possible; otherwise the trout may be long gone by the time the fly hits the water. Sometimes, fish will continue rising at or near the same spot—usually a sign of a feeding school that's in no hurry to move on—but when a rise is not repeated, then it's always advisable to look for other rises farther down the beach—a sure sign that a school is on the move.

Anglers experienced in fishing freshwater lakes and ponds know the wisdom of "fishing the slicks" on windy days, and the same applies to estuary fishing. The "slicks" are patches of water that remain calm even when a breeze is causing a mild chop everywhere else. These calm patches may be due to vagaries of the wind or currents in the water; in estuaries, they are often the result of tidal currents. Whatever the cause, a dry fly fished in the slicks is always more visible to the fish than one fished in the chop.

If no rises are seen, then one should search for signs of baitfish. Schools of baitfish often reveal their pres-

A double rainbow over Puget Sound.

ence by dimpling the surface, leaving a pattern of little rings almost like raindrops striking the water. When you see this, cutthroat may be lurking nearby, and it may be worth casting an imitation into or near the school of baitfish.

If there is no sign of surface activity at all, then it's best to search the water systematically. Cast in a semicircle until you are satisfied there are no fish about, then move on. Searching with a wet fly sometimes pays off, but a dry fly is almost always more effective. By covering the water thoroughly with a dry fly and keeping it moving, you will raise many fish whose presence you did not suspect, and many more than you can find with any other method. If rises fail to result in hook-ups, then change the speed of the retrieve until fish begin taking the dry fly firmly. Remember the best results come from casting downtide or downwind.

Perhaps the only time a wet fly is more effective than a dry fly as a searching pattern is when cutthroat are feeding on baitfish. These are the only circumstances when they show anything approaching selectivity, and they may sometimes refuse a fly that does not resemble the baitfish they are feeding on. The type of baitfish varies by season—Pacific sand lance during summer, stickleback in fall, candlefish in winter, small sculpin at almost any season. Other baitfish, such as herring, anchovy, capelin, or smelt, also are taken when available.

Baitfish are most important in the diets of larger sea-run cutthroat. But true shrimp, amphipods, and pillbugs are important, too, especially during fall and winter months, and while cutthroat rarely feed selectively on these organisms, an appropriate imitation works well. I rarely tire of fishing a dry fly, but on occasions when the dry-fly fishing simply seemed too easy I have switched to a shrimp or amphipod imitation as a change of pace, usually with good results.

With most baitfish imitations, a rapid, erratic retrieve works best. Shrimp and amphipod patterns should be fished with a slow retrieve, close to the bottom, perhaps with an occasional fast strip. Pillbugs work best when allowed to drift with the tide, but sometimes a slow retrieve also pays off.

The most important thing to remember in sea-run cutthroat fishing is to start close to shore, right at the water's edge, and begin casting farther out only if you find nothing in the shallows. Pilings, floats, or other structures should not be overlooked; many times on bright, sunlit days when fish were otherwise scarce I have found them holding in the shadows of a float or a dock.

Remember, too, that most sea-run cutthroat found from Puget Sound northward are wild fish, among the very last wild trout we have. Their runs are small, their spawning streams easily damaged, their habitat requirements easily compromised—all good reasons why you should release every one you catch.

Fly Patterns

Suggested wet-fly patterns for Puget Sound or Hood Canal include the Tarboo Special in green, red, or lime, the Fry Fly, or any similar streamer-type baitfish imitation. Others include Knudson's Spider, the Retiary, the

Anglers fishing for winter steelhead near the mouth of a small stream flowing into Hood Canal.

Golden Shrimp and variations, and pillbug patterns in appropriate colors. Murray's Rolled Muddler, a sculpin imitation, and the American Coachman are favorites in British Columbia waters. The Spruce has been an Oregon favorite many years.

Other traditional wet-fly "attractor" patterns, whose dressings are so well known and widely published that I have chosen not to repeat them here, include the Skykomish Sunrise, Brad's Brat, Purple Joe, and Dead Chicken.

The Cutthroat Candy is the dry fly I use most often for sea-runs and other estuarine fish, although any high-floating pattern made of deer or elk hair should do the trick if kept moving. The Humpy and small versions of the Bomber, a deerhair pattern originally developed for Atlantic salmon, also have caught fish in the estuaries.

WINTER STEELHEAD

Season

Mid-December through March, with January usually best. Steelhead kelts are often found in the estuaries in March and April.

Water Type

Unlike salmon, steelhead come into the estuaries on a rising tide and then stubbornly remain for as long as they can when the tide goes out. Usually they are invisible to anglers until a low tide reveals them schooled up in deeper tidewater pools; these schools move about swiftly, sometimes entering water so shallow their passage is marked by ripples on the surface. Anglers wearing polarized lenses can often see these schools swimming in the shallows. At low tide during hours of morning or evening low light, steelhead sometimes rise freely in the estuaries, although their rises are often subtle and may sometimes be mistaken for those of cutthroat or resident coho.

Tides

An outgoing tide with a low near zero or even a minus value is best, and low-water slack is prime time.

Tactics

Look for traveling schools in tidal pools or along gently sloping beaches at low tide. Schools in shallow water are wary in daylight, but usually not as difficult to approach as schools of chum or pink salmon; try to anticipate the direction of travel and get your fly in front of the advancing school. Use an intermediate or slow-sinking line with a wet fly and retrieve it very rapidly. During hours of low light, look for individual rising fish; when you see one, cover it as quickly as possible and begin a rapid retrieve. A wet fly works best, but a skated dry also will draw some spectacular rises. However, steelhead often only bump or splash a skated dry without really trying to take it.

Since management agencies typically devote the output of their hatcheries to only the largest rivers, it bears emphasizing that steelhead returning to smaller streams are usually wild fish. Their runs are often small and extremely fragile and must be protected at all costs. The importance of this cannot be overstated; I know of some little streams with winter steelhead runs sometimes numbering fewer than a couple of dozen fish, so the loss of even one could jeopardize the future of the run. Anglers who fish estuaries for winter steelhead should be prepared to handle any steelhead they hook as carefully as possible, and release every one unharmed.

Fly Patterns

In my experience, winter steelhead in estuaries respond best to a bright, hot-orange fly. I have caught more of them on the Retiary than any other pattern, although I think any fly of similar color would do.

SEA-RUN DOLLY VARDEN

Seasons

April and May are the best months to find these fish in the estuaries.

Water Type

My experience with these fish is limited, but I have found them intermingled with sea-run cutthroat in the same types of water where cutthroat are normally encountered.

Tides

I have most often found sea-run Dollies active on rising tides.

Tactics

The same wet-fly tactics used for sea-run cutthroat work for Dolly Varden. Appropriate baitfish or attractor patterns are both effective.

Dolly Varden are definitely not known as free-rising fish, but I have taken smaller sea-run Dollies on dry flies, fished as one would fish them for sea-run cutthroat.

Fly Patterns

Standard baitfish imitations such as the Tarboo Special, Candlefish, Murray's Rolled Muddler, Fry Fly, or sand lance imitations, or any of the traditional wet-fly attractor patterns already mentioned, work well on sea-run Dolly Varden. The Cutthroat Candy or other dry-fly patterns previously mentioned will work when a floating pattern is indicated.

SEA PERCH

Season

Striped sea perch, pile perch, and black sea perch are the three species of primary interest to fly fishers. Striped sea perch are available year-around in sheltered estuaries from Southeast Alaska to Baja California; the range of the pile perch is similar, but its season is limited from May or June through November. The black sea perch, found from San Francisco Bay southward, is available throughout the year. The redtail surfperch, more commonly sought in the ocean surf, enters the estuaries in summer to spawn and may be taken by fly fishers at that time, particularly in Oregon waters.

Water Type

Schools of sea perch are found in shallow protected bays and estuaries over virtually any type of bottom; pile perch, as their name indicates, like to congregate around clusters of pilings, especially those driven into rocky or cobbled bottoms.

Tides

High tides are best if only because they bring perch into shallow water, close to shore, where they may be more easily reached by fly fishers.

Tactics

Shrimp or scud imitations fished on a sinking line with a slow retrieve near the bottom are highly effective for sea perch. While they do not normally feed on other fish, I have also caught sea perch occasionally on small baitfish imitations. The best fishing is in shallow water, preferably shallow enough that an angler can see the schools of perch as they move around. At one time such schools were common in Puget Sound and Hood Canal, and often they were large enough to be seen from considerable distance; now that perch are less common in these waters, schools are far more difficult to locate.

Once or twice I have seen striped sea perch rise to a dry fly fished dead drift, but these appear to be fluke occurrences and a dry fly is not recommended for these fish.

Fly Patterns

Suggested fly patterns include the Golden Shrimp and variations in colors such as tan or dark olive. The Tarboo Special in red or green also may be effective, especially on pile perch. Most perch have small mouths, so patterns should be in smaller sizes.

ROCKFISH

Season

Copper, quillback, and brown rockfish are the species most often encountered by estuary anglers. All are available year-around but are most accessible to fly fishers during the summer when they enter shallower waters.

Rockfish always have been an important target

species for anglers along the Oregon Coast, and the disappearance of sea-run cutthroat and the decline of many salmon runs have made them even more important; in recognition of that, the Oregon Department of Fish and Wildlife recently reduced the bag limit on these fish. The department in conjunction with Oregon State University also has published a pocket-sized pamphlet called the *Black Rockfish Identification Guide* to help anglers accurately identify different species. The pamphlet, available free, also explains the importance of conserving these fish.

Water type

As befits their name, rockfish prefer to gather around rocky reefs or rock piles in fairly deep water during the winter. In summer months they are found over rocky reefs in shallower water, or in eelgrass beds or kelp forests. During hours of darkness they often move in close to seawalls or jetties to feed. Years ago, when they were still abundant in Puget Sound, I could catch them from the sea wall in front of my home on late summer evenings; unfortunately, that fishing now appears to be a thing of the past.

During daylight hours, rockfish normally are found in open water, usually at depths greater than those frequented by most estuarine species. Since the Oregon coast has limited estuarine habitat, rockfish are most often sought there in open, offshore waters.

Tides

High tides during hours of twilight or darkness sometimes bring rockfish within range of anglers fishing from jetties or from small boats near shore. At other times the best fishing for rockfish is in open waters, where the stage of the tide usually matters little.

Tactics

In open waters, an extra-fast sinking line or shooting head capable of getting the fly down to depths of 30 or 40 feet is often needed. Lines of this type also usually require bigger, heavier rods than any mentioned so far. For shallower waters, a slower-sinking, wet-tip or even intermediate line may be sufficient, especially during hours of darkness. Any of these lines also should suffice when rockfish come to the surface, as they do at times, usually in open water. At whatever depth they are found, the common technique is to cast, let the fly settle to the desired depth, then begin the retrieve, varying both the retrieve and the depth until an effective combination is found.

Remember that the spines of the dorsal, ventral, and anal fins of rockfish are mildly venomous to humans and care should be taken to avoid contact with them.

A sailboat rides at anchor on a foggy winter morning in Hood Canal, near Belfair.

Fly Patterns

Since small fish are the primary food of rockfish, bait-fish patterns are most effective, but they should be larger and heavier than those used for most estuarine gamefish. Again, the Deceiver in appropriate sizes is a good generic pattern for these fish. Steve Probasco's Halfarabbit fly is another pattern that works well on rockfish.

Other Species

Pacific cod are sometimes taken in northern estuaries, although their numbers have declined substantially in the past two decades. The usual season for these fish is from late winter until midsummer. During this time they come into shallow water over rocky bottoms on high tides, most often during hours of darkness, when they sometimes congregate in areas illuminated by electric lights on piers. Small baitfish imitations, including all those previously mentioned, work well at such times.

While the starry flounder is almost without virtue as a gamefish, it is commonly encountered in estuaries. It prefers sandy or muddy bottoms in shallow water, where it can easily take advantage of its shape and natural camouflage. The stage of tide doesn't seem to matter much; if there is any water at all, you can find starry flounder—and where you find one, you will often find many. Should you wish to catch them, an amphipod or shrimp imitation retrieved slowly on a slow-sinking or intermediate line is usually effective. Even more deadly is to let the fly sink all the way to the bottom so it kicks up a little puff of silt with each pull of the retrieve; flounder can hardly resist such a sight.

Ling cod, cabezon, and kelp greenling are sometimes taken by fly fishers seeking rockfish around kelp beds or rocky reefs and the same techniques and fly patterns used for rockfish also work for these species.

From time to time other marine species will come to an estuary angler's fly, but mostly these are taken incidentally by fishermen seeking something else. These fish—Pacific halibut, English sole, walleye pollack, and others—have yet to develop any popular following, so anglers have given little thought to tactics or fly patterns designed to take them. This may change as interest grows in estuary fly fishing, and certainly there are many opportunities for enterprising, innovative anglers.

Tactics and Ethics

In at least one important sense, fly-fishing tactics and ethics are inseparable. To adopt the one is to accept the other—that is, to take up fly fishing and subject one's self to its inherent rules and limitations is in itself acceptance of a form of ethical behavior. So any angler willing to embrace the self-imposed handicaps that are an essential part of fly fishing should have no difficulty adopting the ethical precepts necessary for angling, particularly estuary fly fishing, to exist and survive in a modern context.

These are: Respect for the fish, for the habitat that sustains and nurtures the fish, and all the other myriad forms of life that occupy and share that habitat; respect for the rights of others, including property owners and other anglers; and respect for the sport and all its traditions and values. But most of all, respect for the fish and their habitat.

This means: Knowing and abiding by the fishing regulations for any given area—all the regulations, not just those that seem reasonable or convenient to follow. It means handling each fish with care and releasing every wild fish taken, without exception, and encouraging others to do likewise. And it means doing whatever is possible and necessary, either as a private citizen or member of an organized angling group, to help preserve habitat and promote conservation.

There should be no debate about any of this. Those who use or exploit a resource in any way, even the most innocent or noncomsumptive way, have a moral responsibility for its stewardship and safekeeping. Considering the fragile nature of estuaries and the extent to which they already have been abused, that responsibility is especially clear for anglers who choose to fish in the estuaries. Nearly every species of estuarine fish—transient or resident, quick or slow, spectacular or ordinary—is now at risk. Widespread habitat destruction coupled with the constantly increasing pressures of commercial and sport fisheries and a host of other problems have forced many stocks near or even past the point of extinction, and there is no reason to feel complacent about the safety of those remaining. So the price of membership in the clan of estuary fly fishers includes accepting the responsibility to do one's share to protect the resource where it still exists and to work for its restoration where it has been damaged.

The peculiar ambience of Northwest estuaries offers a type of fly fishing unique in all the world. The estuaries, the mountains and forests that rise around them, and the countless numbers of fish, birds, animals, and plants that live in them, are integral parts of the Northwest heritage. Here, in the estuaries, the rivers come home to the sea; here, life first left the sea and ventured onto land, and here we are inescapably drawn—not just as anglers or observers, but also as members of the complex web of life that extends from the estuaries to the far corners of the sea and the far reaches of the land.

Here, where fresh and salt waters meet, there are marvels and mysteries beyond measure, opportunities to explore the unknown and to experience the deepest rhythms of life; and here also is the promise of infinite rewards. Let us resolve that these wonderful wild places shall never be allowed to pass away.

The assortment of fly patterns listed here and in the previous chapter includes those in which I have confidence based on personal experience, or which have been recommended by other anglers whose knowledge and judgment I trust. It includes a few more or less "generic" dressings—or as close to generic as one can get in this type of fishing—plus a few others not yet well known but which I have found to have merit.

Of the 25 patterns listed, only four are dry flies. That seems ironic, given that I now probably fish dry flies in the estuaries more than 80 percent of the time, and the proportion of wet patterns to dries given here is almost exactly the opposite of that. But the notion of dry-fly fishing in estuaries is new and still in the process of acceptance and most anglers still rely upon wet-fly patterns, so this proportion is probably correct for the present.

Of the 25 patterns, 15 clearly fall into the category of "attractor" flies, intended to capture the attention of fish by their color and flash or—in the case of dry flies—by their movement on the surface. Of the 10 more-or-less imitative patterns listed, the majority are intended to mimic baitfish, but even some of these are all-purpose flies, not meant to resemble a particular species. I believe

this proportion of attractor to imitative patterns also is probably correct given the current state of fly tiers' efforts to apply the science of "exact imitation" to estuary fishing. Those efforts are still in their infancy, and the opportunity to develop new and better imitations of estuarine baitfish, shrimp, amphipods, isopods, and other organisms represents an exciting opportunity for innovative fly tiers.

Some of the patterns on this list are my own, and one was developed by my son, Randy. I suppose that was inevitable, considering we are no different from the majority of estuary fly fishers, most of whom tie and favor their own patterns. I claim no special cachet for any of these flies, other than that I am satisfied of their worth from having fished them many years; otherwise they are probably no better or worse than any other patterns offered here. I do hope they will offer some useful ideas to other tiers, just as they were partly inspired by the work of others. Perhaps a few years down the road some of them will come back to me in different form, and I shall be able to take advantage of improvements added by others. That is how things should work, and how fly patterns should evolve.

Here is the list of 25 recommended patterns:

Alaskabou

Hook: Sizes 2/0-4.
Tying thread: Fluorescent red.
Wing: Fluorescent chartreuse marabou.
Topping: Several strands of Krystal Flash.
Hackle: White.
Comment: While the chartreuse version is most popular for chum, coho, and pink salmon, other popular combinations of this no-body pattern include fluorescent pink and white, or hot orange and purple.

American Coachman

Hook: Sizes 4-8.
Tying thread: Black.
Tail: Red calf tail.
Body: Yellow wool.
Wing: White polar bear hair, calf tail, or buck tail.
Hackle: Brown, tied wet and full.
Comment: The American Coachman, once popular throughout the Northwest as an "attractor" pattern for sea-run cutthroat, is still used widely in British Columbia. However, when someone recommends this fly there's no assurance he or she means exactly the pattern given here. There are countless variations of this pattern, so many that the original dressing seems to have become lost, and the fly is no longer commonly listed in pattern books. The dressing given here is the one most familiar to me, but I make no claim that it represents the "original" pattern.

Bomber (Sea-Run Cutthroat Version) (dry)

Hook: Size 8-10 low-water Atlantic salmon hook.
Tying thread: Black.
Body: Dark deer body hair, clipped to a cylindrical or cigar shape.
Hackle: Black or dark brown, dry-fly quality, palmered over the full length of the body.
Comment: This pattern is a smaller variation of the dressing developed for Atlantic salmon fishing. Skated rapidly over the surface, it makes an effective dry fly for sea-run cutthroat in the estuaries. Resident coho also respond to this pattern.

Candlefish

Hook: Sizes 2-4.
Tying thread: Black.
Body: Cut a length of transparent pearlescent mylar tubing about 2 1/2 times the length of the hook shank and remove the core. Insert a length of red or pink Amnesia or similar monofilament leader material inside the tubing. Then work the tubing onto the hook and secure it along with the monofilament about a quarter of an inch behind the eye of the hook.
Tail: Cut a V-shaped section from a length of brown hen hackle and insert it into the rear end of the mylar tubing so that the long fibers extend outward as a tail. Apply super glue and crimp the tubing around the hackle until the glue sets up.
Wing: Dark blue dyed bucktail, sparse, about half the length of the mylar tubing.
Eyes: Yellow with black pupils.
Comment: Several different patterns have been designed to imitate the eulachon or candlefish, *Thaleichthys*
pacificus, but this one—developed by the staff of the Northwest Angler Fly Shop in Poulsbo, Washington—strikes me as one of the best. (See also the Lambuth Candlefish.)

Chum Candy

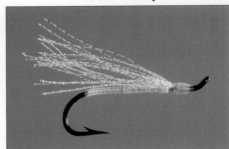

Hook: Sizes 4-6.
Tying thread: Chartreuse.
Body: Chartreuse floss, thin.
Wing: Chartreuse Krystal Flash.
Comment: There are several variations of the Chum Candy; the one given here is easy to tie and makes an effective pattern for chum salmon fished either dead drift or with a very slow retrieve. It also sometimes works for coho in the inner estuaries. Another variation of this fly calls for a tail of chartreuse-dyed marabou, a body of chartreuse chenille, and sparsely tied chartreuse hackle.

Cutthroat Candy (dry)

Hook: Size 8, 2X fine wire.
Tying thread: Tan monocord.
Body: Deer hair, clipped to a cylindrical shape.
Hackle: Chocolate brown, palmered.
Wing: Deer hair.
Comment: This is the dry-fly pattern I use most often for cutthroat. It has its origins in the "Salmon Candy" series of dry flies originated by Lloyd Frese for landlocked Atlantic salmon in Hosmer Lake, Oregon. Following some of Lloyd's ideas, I first tied this fly with a brown wool body and a deer hair overlay, but found it did not float well when the wool became waterlogged. Several years ago I changed the dressing, giving up the wool body for one of clipped deer hair, and abandoning the overlay while still keeping a deer hair wing. The result is a fly that floats better, even when skated over the surface for long periods.

Deceiver

Hook: Sizes 4/0-2.
Tying thread: Black.
Tail: A pair of white saddle hackles tied in near the bend of the hook and extending to the rear for a distance at least equal to the full length of the hook shank.
Body: Silver mylar tinsel.
Collar: White bucktail.
Wing: Dyed dark blue bucktail or polar bear hair topped with a half dozen strands of peacock sword.
Beard: Dyed red bucktail, short.
Eyes: White with black pupils.
Comment: The Deceiver is really more a style of tying than an individual pattern, and there are many variations. The version shown here is a long way from Lefty Kreh's original, which calls for at least six and sometimes as many as 12 white saddle hackles for the tail, wing, and body of the fly. Often these are mixed with flash material like Flashabou or Krystal Flash. Chartreuse, rather than blue, is frequently used as topping for the wing. However tied, the Deceiver is a useful generic baitfish imitation for Pacific salmon, rockfish, or other marine species in Northwest estuaries.

Fry Fly

Hook: Size 4, long shank.
Tying thread: Red.
Body and tail: Braided silver mylar tubing with core removed. The tubing is slipped over the hook shank and secured fore and aft with tying thread, leaving perhaps a half inch of tubing extending rearward beyond the after tie. The individual strands of this half-inch of tubing are picked out to form the tail.

Beard: White polar bear, bucktail, or artificial substitute
Wing: Black bucktail, sparse, extending twice the length of the hook and enclosing several strands of red and green Krystal Flash.
Head: The white hair used in the beard and the black hair used in the wing are brought forward together and tied off behind the eye of the hook, leaving the excess extending forward over the eye. The excess then is gathered and pulled back to form a round, blunt head about a quarter inch long. This is secured by a second tie and any remaining excess hair is trimmed away. The result, if done properly, is a neat rounded head, and the rear tie of red thread that holds the head in place also simulates gills. The head is coated thoroughly with tying cement, allowed to dry, stick-on eyes are applied, and another coat of cement is applied.
Comment: An effective small baitfish imitation, this pattern is used by anglers for sea-run cutthroat and coho around Discovery Bay, Port Townsend, and along the beaches of the Strait of Juan de Fuca.

Golden Shrimp

Hook: Sizes 10-12.
Tying thread: Tan monocord.
Hackle: Ginger, with fibers stripped from one side of the quill. Tie in the hackle tip at the bend of the hook to form the tail of the fly and let the rest of the feather hang free while you apply the ribbing and body material.
Rib: Fine gold wire.
Body: Golden olive floss, thickest near the bend of the hook, tapering forward toward the eye. When you have completed wrapping the body, bring forward the remaining portion of the hackle feather and place it along the belly of the fly so that the hackle fibers hang down to form the legs of the shrimp. Secure the hackle with the fine gold wire, using a dubbing needle to keep individual hackle fibers from being bound under the ribbing. Then take the long fibers remaining at the base of the hackle, extend them for

ward over the eye of the hook, and secure them with tying thread to serve as antennae.
Comment: Another of my own patterns, this one originally was developed as a freshwater scud imitation for Kamloops trout in British Columbia. Later I also found it to be an effective imitation for *Anisogammarus*, the scud-like amphipod found in estuaries, which are a favorite food of sea-run cutthroat, sea perch, starry flounder, and other species. Variations of this pattern, also effective for estuary fishing, include tying the fly with a body of olive drab, gray, or pink floss, with the hackle and tying thread matched to the body color. The tying thread is used as ribbing in these variations, rather than gold wire.

Green Weenie

Hook: Sizes 4-6.
Tying thread: Fluorescent green.
Tail: Red hackle fibers.
Body: Fluorescent green chenille.
Rib: Embossed silver tinsel.
Hackle: White, tied sparsely.
Wing: Natural white polar bear hair or artificial substitute.
Comment: This is one of several patterns bearing the same unfortunate name. Another version calls for a body of silver diamond braid with a shoulder of fluorescent green or chartreuse chenille, chartreuse hackle, and silver bead-chain eyes. All the Green Weenie patterns are effective for chum salmon and occasionally for other species.

Halfarabbit

Hook: Size 3/0 or 2/0.
Tying thread: Red.

Tail: Take an eight-inch strip of white rabbit fur, or rabbit fur dyed rust color, and secure one end to the hook shank so that the other end extends to the rear of the hook. Cut the strip about three inches beyond the bend, leaving a three-inch tail. Tie in about a dozen strands of Holographic Fly Fiber on top of the tail, trimming it to the same length as the rabbit fur.

Body: Take the remainder of the original strip of rabbit fur, secure it to the hook shank just in front of the tail, and wrap it forward around the hook to serve as the body of the fly. Trim away any excess.

Comment: This pattern, developed by Steve Probasco, is quick and easy to tie. It has proven its worth on rockfish.

Humpy (dry)

Hook: Size 8, 2X fine wire.
Tying thread: Tan or brown.
Tail: Dark deer hair, equal to the length of the hook.
Body and wing: Dark deer hair, thick, tied in at the midpoint of the hook shank with the tips extending rearward. The hair is then pulled forward to form a thick, rounded shellback, which is tied down at the front of the hook, leaving the tips of the hair extending forward beyond the eye of the hook. These are then pulled back and tied upright and divided to form the wing of the fly.
Hackle: Grizzly and brown mixed.
Comment: Also sometimes called the Goofus Bug, this fly's name is derived from its shape and has nothing to do with humpbacked (pink) salmon. Because it is made mostly of deer hair, the fly floats extremely well and has a high profile that makes it easy to see on the water. These qualities make it an excellent dry fly for sea-run cutthroat when it is skated over the surface in estuaries.

Humpy Hooker

Hook: Sizes 6-10 standard Atlantic salmon hook.
Tying thread: Hot pink.
Tag: Silver tinsel.
Tail: Hot pink marabou.
Body: Hot pink yarn.
Ribbing: Silver tinsel.
Wing: Hot pink marabou.
Comment: This fly is about as pink as it gets—and pink is the favorite color of pink salmon, or humpbacks, from which the fly's name is derived.

Knudson's Spider

Hook: Sizes 4-6.
Tying thread: Black.
Body: Yellow chenille, medium to full.
Hackle: Three or four turns of barred mallard breast, very long and full.
Comment: This old standby was created by the late Al Knudson of Everett, Washington. The original version also apparently included several turns of grizzly hackle behind the barred mallard breast, but the grizzly hackle usually is omitted from modern versions. Sometimes a tail of barred mallard breast is added. The standard pattern is useful as an attractor fly for sea-run cutthroat, but I have also had success with resident coho using emerald green chenille for the body and dyed green mallard breast for the hackle.

Lambuth's Candlefish

Hook: Sizes 2/0-4 extra-long shank.
Tying thread: Black.
Body: Silver tinsel.
Wing: First tie in an underwing of mixed pale blue and green dyed polar bear hair; top this with a thin layer of dyed red polar bear hair; top this with a layer of mixed dyed blue and olive green polar bear hair. The full wing should be long, tied in streamer fashion.
Comment: The late Letcher Lambuth, innovative Seattle rodmaker, fly tier, and angler, developed this pattern after studying live candlefish (*Thaleichthys pacificus*) in a saltwater aquarium under different lighting conditions. Tied properly, it has a long, thin silhouette in the water, suggesting the real thing. The original pattern was conceived in the 1930s; modern versions often substitute artificial hair for polar bear and braided mylar tubing for the silver tinsel.

Lime Green Woolly Bugger

Hook: Sizes 6-10 standard Atlantic salmon hook.
Tying thread: Lime green.
Tail: Lime green marabou mixed with several strands of green or clear Krystal Flash.
Body: Lime green chenille.
Hackle: Lime green, palmered, fuller toward the head of the fly.
Comment: Dressed in the same manner as the popular freshwater pattern of the same name, the only thing different about this Woolly Bugger is its color, which makes it an effective fly for chum and coho salmon in the estuaries.

Murray's Rolled Muddler

Hook: Sizes 10-12 long shank.
Tying thread: Red.
Tail: Barred mallard flank, rolled.
Body: Silver tinsel.
Rib: Oval silver tinsel, wrapped in a reverse spiral.
Wing: Barred mallard flank, rolled.
Head: Deer hair, trimmed Muddler-fashion to an arrow shape, leaving four or five strands to extend backward and blend with the wing.
Comment: Developed by Tom Murray, this pattern is widely used as a small sculpin imitation by British Columbia sea-run cutthroat anglers. Some tiers wrap the red tying thread both fore and aft of the head, with the after wrap intended to simulate the gills of a sculpin.

Pink Eve

Hook: Size 2.
Tying thread: Pink.
Tail: Fluorescent pink FisHair.
Body: Oval silver tinsel.
Wing: Fluorescent pink FisHair.
Comment: This pattern, created by Barry Thornton, is growing in popularity as a taker of pink salmon.

Pink Shrimp

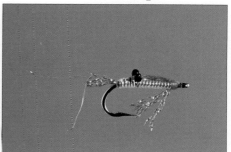

Hook: Sizes 8-14.
Tying thread: Pink
Underbody: Silver mylar tinsel.
Overbody: Pink V-rib.
Eyes: Black monofilament tied on top of the body, a little more than halfway back from the eye of the hook.
Overlay: About a half dozen strands of pearlescent pink Krystal Flash or similar material. Allow strands at the rear to extend about a third of an inch past the bend of the hook to serve as the tail; those at the front should be tied down and under the hook as a beard. The beard should be about a half-inch long.
Comment: One of many euphasid shrimp imitations, useful when coho are feeding on these organisms in open water.

Pillbug

Hook: Size 10-14, weighted with lead wire wrapped around the shank.
Tying thread: Brown or gray, matching body material.
Body: Brown, olive or gray mohair, picked out underneath.
Comment: A very small, simple imitation to use when sea-run cutthroat are feeding on isopods, or pillbugs. In larger sizes tied in brown or olive, this pattern is a reasonable imitation of the pillbug *Idotea wosnesenskii*; in smaller sizes tied in gray it matches the pillbug *Gnorimosphaeroma oregonensis*. Both are taken in large numbers by sea-run cutthroat; in fact, I have found more pill-bugs in sea-run cutthroat stomach samples than anything else. The weighted hook is necessary to get the fly down to the level where it should be fished.

Pink Polliwog (dry)

Hook: 1/0-4, short shank.
Tying thread: Fluorescent pink.
Tail: Fluorescent pink marabou, long and full, enclosing several thin strips of mylar in matching color.
Head: Deer hair dyed fluorescent pink, tied full and thick, trimmed flat on the bottom and wedge-shaped on top, almost like a deer hair popper or slider. On a 1/0 hook, the head should be at least an inch long.
Comment: This is a "dry" pattern used primarily for chum salmon in Alaska; it also works on coho and pink salmon. The technique is to cast the fly over a school of rolling, porpoising salmon, give it a single long strip, then let it sit long enough for the marabou tail to sink down into the water, then give it another long strip and repeat the process.

Randy's Retiary

Hook: Sizes 4-6 standard Atlantic salmon hook.
Tying thread: Black or hot orange.
Tail: Hot orange marabou.
Body: Hot orange chenille.
Rib: Silver tinsel.
Wing: Hot orange marabou.
Comment: This pattern was developed by my son, Randy, and is the best fly I know for winter steelhead in the estuaries. It also works well for sea-run cutthroat, coho, and other species of salmon; in fact, I have probably caught more different species of fish on this fly than any other.

Sand Lance

Hook: Sizes 4-6 long shank.
Tying thread: Black.
Body: Gold mylar or Holographic Fly Fiber.
Wing: Tie in a half-dozen strands of clear Krystal Flash topped by a thin layer of polar bear hair dyed blue gray and top with 10-12 strands of peacock herl. The wing should be twice the length of the body.
Eyes: White or red with black pupils.
Comment: A good imitation of the sand lance *(Ammodytes hexapterus)* is necessary for fishing resident coho salmon in the estuaries, especially during summer months; it also works well for sea-run cutthroat at times.

Spruce

Hook: Sizes 6-10 long shank.
Tying thread: Black.

Tail: Half a dozen strands of peacock sword, short.
Body: Rear third red floss; forward two thirds peacock herl.
Wing: A pair of cream badger hackles tied back to back and extending rearward to a point slightly beyond the tail of the fly.
Hackle: Matching cream badger hackle tied wet and full.
Comment: A traditional sea-run cutthroat "attractor" pattern, still popular in Oregon waters.

Tarboo Special

Hook: Sizes 4-6 standard Atlantic salmon hook.
Tying thread: Black or dark green.
Body and tail: Braided silver mylar tubing, core removed, bound to the shank fore and aft. Leave about a half inch of extra tubing behind the after tie and pick out individual strands of the mylar braid to form the tail.
Wing: Tie in an underwing of natural cream or white polar bear or substitute, then add an overwing of dyed green polar bear or mixed blue and green polar bear or substitute.
Eyes: Stick-on eyes, white with black pupils, optional.
Comment: This is my own pattern, a sort of all-purpose baitfish imitation. The version with the mixed green-and-blue wing makes a reasonable imitation of the stickleback, *Gasterosteus aculeatus.* I also tie this pattern with blue, red, or lime-colored wings. It is quick and easy to tie and quite durable. In its various color combinations I have found it effective at times for sea-run cutthroat, adult coho, resident coho, sea perch, and other species.

I do not think any estuary fly fisher will go very far wrong by limiting his or her fly selection to these 25 patterns, or a representative sample of them. There are many others to choose from, however, and their dressings will be found in the fly-tying titles listed in the bibliography.

I. Books

Alaska Flyfishers (Dirk V. Derksen, editor). *Fly Patterns of Alaska*; Frank Amato Publications, Inc. Portland, OR., 1993.

Bearman, Gerry, editor. *Waves, Tides and Shallow-Water Processes*; Pergamon Press, Oxford, England, 1989.

Behnke, Robert J. *Native Trout of Western North America*; American Fisheries Society, Bethesda, MD., Monograph No. 6, 1992.

Davey, Alfred G. (editor). *The Gilly: A Flyfisher's Guide to British Columbia*; Kelowna, B.C., 1985.

Emory, K.O., and Aubrey, David G. *Sea Levels, Land Levels, and Tide Gauges*; Springer-Verlag, New York and Berlin, 1991.

Ferguson, Bruce; Johnson, Les; and Trotter, Pat. *Fly Fishing for Pacific Salmon*; Frank Amato Publications, Inc. Portland, OR., 1985.

Goodson, Gar. Fishes of the Pacific Coast; Stanford University Press, Stanford, CA., 1988.

Hellekson, Terry. *Fish Flies, Volume II*; Frank Amato Publications, Inc. Portland, OR., 1995.

Hutchins, Ross E. *Insects*; Prentice-Hall, Inc., Englewood Cliffs, NJ., 1966.

Inland Empire Fly Fishing Club (Fenton Roskelly, editor). *Flies of the Northwest*; Frank Amato Publicatons, Inc. Portland, OR., 1986.

Kozloff, Eugene N. *Seashore Life of Puget Sound, the Strait of Georgia, and the San Juan Archipelago*; University of Washington Press, Seattle, WA., 1973.

Kreh, Lefty. *Saltwater Fly Patterns*; Lyons & Burford, New York, NY., revised edition, 1995.

Kruckeberg, Arthur R. *The Natural History of the Puget Sound Country*; University of Washington Press, Seattle, WA., 1991.

Mann, K.H., and Lazier, J.R.N. *Dyanmics of Marine Ecosystems*; Blackwell Scientific Publications, Boston, MA.

Migdalski, Edward C., and Fichter, George S. *The Fresh & Salt Water Fishes of the World*; Alfred A. Knopf, New York, NY., 1976.

Mitchell, Ed. *Fly Rodding the Coast*; Stackpole Books, Mechanicsburg, PA., 1995.

Patrick, Roy. *Pacific Northwest Fly Patterns*; privately published, Seattle, WA., 1970.

Perrins, Christopher M., and Middleton, Alex L.A., editors. *The Encyclopedia of Birds*; Facts on File Publications, New York, NY., 1985.

Raymond, Steve. *The Year of the Angler*; 1995 edition, Sasquatch Books, Seattle, WA.

Raymond, Steve. *The year of the Trout*; 1995 edition, Sasquatch Books, Seattle, WA.

Ricketts, Edward F., Calvin, Jack, and Hedgpeth, Joel W. *Between Pacific Tides*; Stanford University Press, Stanford, CA., 1985 edition, revised by David W. Phillips.

Roberts, George V., Jr. *A Fly Fisher's Guide to Saltwater Naturals and Their Imitation*; Ragged Mountain Press, Camden, ME., 1994.

Route, Anthony J. *Flyfishing Alaska*; Johnson Books, Boulder, CO., 1989.

Schureman, Paul. *Manual of Harmonic Analysis and Prediction of Tides*; U.S. Department of Commerce, Coast and Geodetic Survey, Special Publication No. 98, reprinted January 1994.

Snively, Gloria. *Exploring the Seashore in British Columbia, Washington and Oregon*; Gordon Soules Book Publishers, West Vancouver, B.C., 9th printing, 1992.

Somerton, David, and Murray, Craig. *Field Guide to the Fish of Puget Sound and the Northwest Coast*; a Washington Sea Grant Publication, distributed by the University of Washington Press, Seattle, WA., 1976.

Steward, Albert N., Dennis, LaRea J., and Gilkey, Helen M. *Aquatic Plants of the Pacific Northwest*; Oregon State University Press, Corvallis, OR., 2nd edition, 1963.

Thomson, Richard E. *Oceanography of the British Columbia Coast*; Canadian Department of Fisheries and Oceans, Ottawa, 1981.

Thornton, Barry M. *Saltwater Fly Fishing for Pacific Salmon*; Hancock, Surrey, B.C., 1995.

Zetler, Bernard D. *Computer Applications to Tides in the National Ocean Survey*; Supplement to Manual of Harmonic Analysis and Prediction of Tides, U.S. Department of Commerce, National Oceanic and Atmospheric Administration, National Ocean Survey, Special Publication No. 98, January 1982.

II. Periodicals and Reports

"A Review of Fish-Habitat Improvement Projects in British Columbia: Do We Know Enough to Do the Right Thing?" by Ron A. Ptolemy, British Columbia Ministry of the Environment, Fisheries Branch, Victoria, B.C.; Sea-Run Cutthroat Trout Symposium, Reedsport, Oregon, 1995.

"A Study of Steelhead-Cutthroat Trout in Alaska," by Darwin E. Jones. Alaska Department of Fish and Game, Research Project Segment, Volume 13, Report No. G-11-1, July 1, 1971-June 30, 1972.

"Baitfish Management Activities in Washington State from July 1, 1974, to December 31, 1975," by Dan Pentilla and Dwane Day. Washington State Department of Fisheries, Progress Report No. 76-02, July 1976.

"Biological Status Review of Umpqua River Sea-Run Cutthroat Trout," by Orlay Johnson, National Marine Fisheries Service, Northwest Fisheries Science Center, Seattle, WA.; Sea-Run Cutthroat Trout Symposium, Reedsport, Oregon, 1995.

Brannon, E.L., and Salo, E.O., editors. Proceedings of the Salmon and Trout Migratory Behavior Symposium; School of Fisheries, University of Washington, Seattle, 1982.

"Canadian Tide and Current Tables, 1994; Volume 5, Juan de Fuca Strait and Strait of Georgia." Canadian Department of Fisheries and Oceans, Ottawa, Canada, 1994.

"Chemical and Biological Survey of Liberty Bay, Washington," by Joseph M. Cummins, et. al. U.S. Environmental Protection Agency, Region X, Seattle, WA., 1976.

"Coastal Cutthroat Trout: A Life History Compendium," by Patrick C. Trotter Transactions of the American Fisheries Society, Vol. 118, 1989; pp. 463-473.

"Effect of Release Size on Return Rates of Hatchery Sea-Run Cutthroat Trout," by Jack Tipping, Washington Department of Game. The Progressive Fish Culturist, Vol. 48, 1986; pp. 195-197.

"The Effects of Interspecific Interactions and Hybridization on Sea-Run Cutthroat Trout," by Denise Hawkins, School of Fisheries, University of Washington, Seattle, WA.; Sea-Run Cutthroat Trout Symposium, Reedsport, Oregon, 1995.

"Estuarine and Saltwater Residence of Sea-Run Cutthroat Trout," by William Pearcy, College of Oceanic and Atmospheric Sciences, Oregon State University, Corvallis, OR.; Sea-Run Cutthroat Trout Symposium, Reedsport, Oregon 1995.

"Evaluation of Stocking Hatchery-Reared Sea-Run Cutthroat Trout in Streams of Hood Canal," by John S. Hisata. Washington State Department of Game, Job Progress Report AFS44-1, May 1970-June 1971.

"Evolution, Systematics, and Structure of *Oncornynchus clarki clarki*," by Robert J. Behnke, Department of Fishery and Wildlife Biology, Colorado State University, Fort Collins, CO.; Sea-Run Cutthroat Trout Symposium, Reedsport, Oregon, 1995.

"Federal Requirements and Safety Tips for Recreational Boats." U.S. Department of Transportation, United States Coast Guard, Washington, D.C. (undated).

"Fish and Wildlife of Willapa Bay, Washington." U.S. Department of the Interior, Fish and Wildlife Service, Portland, OR., 1970.

"Follow that Cutthroat," by Dick Thompson. The Flyfisher, Volume V, Number 4, 1972.

Gresswell, Robert E., editor. Status and Management of Interior Stocks of Cutthroat Trout. American Fisheries Society, Bethesda, MD., Symposium 4, 1988.

"Map Showing Spawning Areas of Anadromous Fish in Southern Hood Canal, Washington," by John D. Findlay. U.S. Geological Survey, Washington, D.C., 1973.

Matthews, Kathleen Ryan. Habitat Use and Movement Patterns of Copper, Quillback, and Brown Rockfishes in Puget Sound, Washington; unpublished doctoral thesis, University of Washington School of Fisheries, Seattle, WA., 1988.

"Migratory Patterns of Mature Cutthroat Trout from Auke Lake and Eva Lake," by Doug Jones and Cheryl Seifert, Alaska Department of Fish and Game, Division of Sport Fish, Douglas, AK.; Sea-Run Cutthroat Trout Symposium, Reedsport, Oregon, 1995.

"Observations on the distribution and activities of rockfish, *Sebastes*., in Saanich Inlet, British Columbia, from the *Pisces IV* Submersible," by Debra J. Murie, Daryl C. Parkyn, Bruce G. Clapp and Geoffrey G. Krause. Fishery Bulletin, U.S. Department of Commerce, Seattle, WA.; Volume 92, Number 2, April 1994; pp. 313-323.

"Our Restless Tides," U.S. Department of Commerce, National Ocean and Atmospheric Administration, National Ocean Survey; pamphlet (undated).

"Pile Perch, Striped Seaperch, and Rubberlip Seaperch," by Ronald A. Fritzsche and Thomas J. Hassler. Species Profiles: Life Histories and Environmental Requirements of Coastal Fishes and Invertebrates, Biological Report 82, Fish and Wildlife Service, U.S. Department of the Interior, Coastal Ecology Group, U.S. Army Corps of Engineers; July, 1989.

"Population Dynamics and Life History Aspects of Native Coastal Cutthroat Trout Populations," by R.D. Giger. State of Oregon, Research Project No. F-72-R-4, July 1, 1967-June 30, 1968.

"Population Structure: A Coastwide Genetic Survey of Coastal Cutthroat Trout," by Thomas H. Williams, Department of Fisheries and Wildlife, Oregon State University, Corvallis, OR.; Kenneth P. Currens, Northwest Indian Fisheries Commmission, Olympia, WA.; and Gordon H. Reeves, U.S. Forest Service, Forestry Sciences Laboratory, Corvallis, OR.; Sea-Run Cutthroat Trout Symposium, Reedsport, Oregon, 1995.

"The Role of Land Management: Past, Present, and Future," by Gordon H. Reeves, U.S. Forest Service, Forestry Sciences Laboratory, Corvallis, OR.; Sea-Run Cutthroat Trout Symposium, Reedsport, Oregon, 1995.

"The Role of Organized Angling Groups in Recovery of Cutthroat Trout," by Dave Schorsch, Sea-Run Cutthroat Trout Coalition, Sumner, WA., and Joseph Jaquet, South Sound Flyfishers, Olympia, WA.; Sea-Run Cutthroat Trout Symposium, Reedsport, Oregon, 1995.

"The Role of Special Angling Regulations in Maintaining and Rebuilding Populations of Sea-Run Cutthroat Trout," by Roger D. Harding, Alaska Department of Fish and Game, Division of Sport Fish, Douglas, AK., and Robert E. Gresswell, U.S. Forest Service, Forestry Sciences Laboratory, Corvallis, OR.; Sea-Run Cutthroat Trout Symposium, Reedsport, Oregon, 1995.

"Safe Boating Guide," Canadian Coast Guard, Ottawa, Canada (undated).

"Salmonid Fishes and the Estuarine Environment," by J. E. Thorpe; *Estuaries*, the Journal of the Estuarine Research Foundation; Vol. 17, No. 1A, March, 1994; pp. 76-93.

"Sea-Run Cutthroat Broodstock Development and Evaluation of a New Enhancement Technique," by James M. Johnston and Stewart P. Mercer. Washington State Department of Game, Fishery Research Report, Olympia, WA., 1977.

"Sea-Run Cutthroat in Saltwater Pens: Broodstock Development and Extended Juvenile Rearing," by James M. Johnston and Stewart P. Mercer. Washington State Department of Game, Fishery Research Report, Olympia, WA., 1976.

"Sea-Run Cutthroat Trout: Life History Profile," by Patrick C. Trotter, Seattle, WA.; Sea-Run Cutthroat Trout Symposium, Reedsport, Oregon, 1995.

Smith, J.L., Bengston, C., and Brown, J. Maintenance Dredging and the Environment of Grays Harbor, Washington; U.S. Army Corps of Engineers.

"Status and Trends of Anadromous Salmonids in the Coastal Zone," by Jack E. Williams, Bureau of Land Management, Intermountain Research Station, Boise, Idaho; Sea-Run Cutthroat Trout Symposium, Reedsport, Oregon, 1995.

"Status of Anadromous Cutthroat Trout in British Columbia," by Tim L. Slaney, Aquatic Resources Ltd., Vancouver, B.C.; Sea-Run Cutthroat Trout Symposium, Reedsport, Oregon, 1995.

"Status of Sea-Run Cutthroat Stocks in Alaska," by Artwin E. Schmidt, Alaska Department of Fish and Game, Sitka, AK.; Sea-Run Cutthroat Trout Symposium, Reedsport, Oregon, 1995.

"Status of Sea-Run Cutthroat Trout in California," by Eric R. Gerstung, California Department of Fish and Game, Inland Fisheries Division, Sacramento; Sea-Run Cutthroat Trout Symposium, Reedsport, Oregon, 1995.

"Status of Sea-Run Cutthroat Trout in Oregon," by Bob Hooton, Oregon Department of Fish and Wildlife, Fish Division, Portland, OR.; Sea-Run Cutthroat Trout Symposium, Reedsport, Oregon, 1995.

"Status of the Sea-Run Cutthroat Trout in Washington," by Steven Leider, Washington Department of Fish and Wildlife, Kalama Research Station, Kelso, WA.; Sea-Run Cutthroat Trout Symposium, Reedsport, Oregon, 1995.

"Steelhead and Sea-Run Cutthroat Trout Life History Study in Southeast Alaska," by D.E. Jones. Alaska Department of Fish and Game, Anadromous Fish Study AFS42-1, Vol. 14, July 1, 1972-June 30, 1973.

"Steelhead and Sea-Run Cutthroat Trout Life History Study in Southeast Alaska," by D.E. Jones. Alaska Department of Fish and Game, Anadromous Fish Study AFS42, Vol. 15, July 1, 1973-June 30, 1974.

"Steelhead and Sea-Run Cutthroat Trout Life History Study in Southeast Alaska," by D.E. Jones. Alaska Department of Fish and Game, Anadromous Fish Study AFS42-3, Vol. 16, July 1, 1974-June 30, 1975.

"Steelhead and Sea-Run Cutthroat Trout Life History Study in Southeast Alaska," by D.E. Jones. Alaska Department of Fish and Game, Anadromous Fish Study AFS42-4, Vol. 17, July 1, 1975-June 30, 1976.

"Tide Tables 1994, High and Low Water Predictions, West Coast of North and South America Including the Hawaiian Islands." U.S. Department of Commerce, National Oceanic and Atmospheric Administration, National Ocean Service, 1994.

"Umpqua Sea-Run Cutthroat Trout: Review of Natural and Human-Caused Factors of Decline." John F. Palmisano, John Palmisano Biological Consultants, Beaverton, OR.; Sea-Run Cutthroat Trout Symposium, Reedsport, Oregon, 1995.

"Water Quality Concerns in Restoration of Stream Habitat in the Umpqua Basin," by Mark Powell, Colliding Rivers Research Inc., Corvallis, OR.; Sea-Run Cutthroat Trout Symposium, Reedsport, Oregon, 1995.

"What Is the Role for Hatchery Programs? The Stone Lagoon Experience," by Eric J. Loudenslager, Department of Fisheries, Humboldt State University, Arcata, CA.; Sea-Run Cutthroat Trout Symposium, Reedsport, Oregon, 1995.

"Where Are We Coming From? A Historic Perspective on Sea-Run Cutthroat Trout," by Phillip W. Schneider, Oregon Fish and Wildlife Commission, Portland, OR.; Sea-Run Cutthroat Trout Symposium, Reedsport, Oregon, 1995.

"Why Sea-Run? An Exploration into the Migratory/Residency Spectrum of Coastal Cutthroat Trout," by Thomas G. Northcote, professor emeritus, University of British Columbia, Vancouver, B.C.; Sea-Run Cutthroat Trout Symposium, Reedsport, Oregon, 1995.

LEARN MORE ABOUT FLY FISHING AND FLY TYING WITH THESE BOOKS

If you are unable to find the books shown below at your local book store
or fly shop you can order direct from the publisher below.

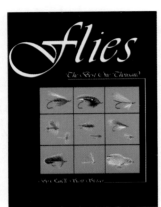

Flies: The Best One Thousand
Randy Stetzer
$24.95

Fly Tying Made Clear and Simple
Skip Morris
$19.95 (HB: $29.95)

The Art of Tying the Dry Fly
Skip Morris
$29.95 (HB: $39.95)

Curtis Creek Manifesto
Sheridan Anderson
$7.95

American Fly Tying Manual
Dave Hughes
$9.95

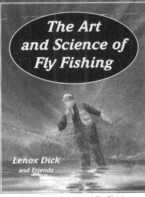

The Art and Science of Fly Fishing
Lenox Dick
$19.95

Western Hatches
Dave Hughes, Rick Hafele
$24.95

Lake Fishing with a Fly
Ron Cordes, Randall Kaufmann
$26.95

Advanced Fly Fishing for Steelhead
Deke Meyer
$24.95

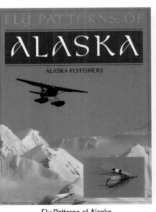

Fly Patterns of Alaska
Alaska Flyfishers
$19.95

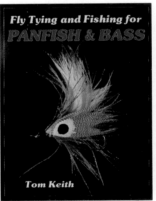

Fly Tying & Fishing for Panfish and Bass
Tom Keith
$19.95

Float Tube Fly Fishing
Deke Meyer
$11.95

VISA, MASTERCARD or AMERICAN EXPRESS ORDERS CALL TOLL FREE: 1-800-541-9498
(9-5 Pacific Standard Time)

Or Send Check or money order to:

Frank Amato Publications
Box 82112
Portland, Oregon 97282

(Please add $3.00 for shipping and handling)